The Stuff Of Legends

Tales of Van Buren Township of
Brown County's People

Helen C. Ayers

Bloomington, IN Milton Keynes, UK

AuthorHouse™
1663 Liberty Drive, Suite 200
Bloomington, IN 47403
www.authorhouse.com
Phone: 1-800-839-8640

AuthorHouse™ UK Ltd.
500 Avebury Boulevard
Central Milton Keynes, MK9 2BE
www.authorhouse.co.uk
Phone: 08001974150

First published by AuthorHouse 11/2/2006

ISBN: 1-4259-6657-8 (sc)

Printed in the United States of America
Bloomington, Indiana

This book is printed on acid-free paper.

Cover Photograph

The picture on the front cover is my mother, Rachel Day. She is a typical portrayal of the women in this book. It appears she might have been making hominy or rendering lard when this picture was taken. Since she does not have a coat on, and lard is usually rendered on very cold days, I assume she was making her yearly supply of hominy. I can see what looks to be a grain of the white corn floating on top of the water.

The picture on the back cover and other illustrations throughout this book were drawn by my friend, George Bredewater, a very talented 80-year-old resident of Van Buren Township. The boy in the box represents my husband when he was a little boy. His father was on Okinawa fighting the Japanese and Mickey wanted to fight also. He learned that the wooden beer box did not make a very stable airplane when he placed it on the tin roof of his mother's house in Story. Read that story inside.

This is a Mike Scovel caricature of George Bredewater. Anyone who knows George will recognize him in this great drawing.

Other Books by Helen Ayers

Appalachian Daughter

And now

The Stuff of Legends

Here is what the readers of Appalachian Daughter have had to say about it:

".....a great read"

".....a delightful book"

".....I laughed and cried all the way through it."

".....some chapters were hilariously funny."

".....I stayed up all night reading it the day I bought it."

".....I could not put it down."

".....it should be made into a movie." (Seven said this)

What is your verdict? Fill out the order blank at the back of this book and find out why they were saying this about Appalachian Daughter.

My Thanks

This book would not have been possible without the cooperation of the surviving family members of the characters in my little stories who provided the photographs used in this book. They also clarified historical data that I needed to make the data correct according to their family records. My heartfelt thanks to all of them for helping me keep the record straight.

I love and have to thank George Bredewater for his amazing artwork and his wife Nancy for helping to keep both of us focused on our chore. George has been my friend for many years and is a very versatile artist.

I have to thank my sons Lonnie and Douglas, whom I seem to mention a lot throughout all my books. They jogged my memory of many little anecdotes I have included in the book about my characters.

And, lastly, thanks to my husband Mickey who provided me with so many little tales about his growing up years here in Van Buren Township.

Preface

The following short stories about the people of Van Buren Township in Brown County Indiana, who shared parts of their daily lives with me, were written to ensure their names would not be forgotten. I consider their names and the little anecdotes about them to be of historical significance and worthy of historical preservation. I have included anecdotes from about sixty of our local families.

The way they lived; the homes they built and the families they reared in the little hamlets like Story and Pike's Peak or Stone Head and Blaneyville and other little hollers and hilltop settlements is indicative of the strong connections these people had with their surroundings.

The story about their schools and churches and the values they learned in both institutions reinforced the positive qualities they were taught at home.

The families I wrote of are not the only families who lived here during the time period I am writing about (1960-2006); there were many others here of course. The omission from this book of those folks does not mean they were of lesser historical importance to the history of this area, because it takes everyone to make any history complete. However, I wrote about only those for whom I had a personal recollection for or who influenced me and my family.

If enough of the remaining families wish me to write about them and publish their family pictures and history I would be glad to do so. That would make a nice addition to this book. They need only to contact me.

Since very early times in our township's history the citizens of Van Buren Township have contributed to the artistic culture of this county in many ways. I have deliberately omitted writing about those talented people who make furniture, pottery, paint or draw pictures and in any other way represent art forms in this book. Their stories will be the subject of my next book, tentatively titled "The Artisans of Van Buren," which I hope to have published by the end of next year.

This period in Van Buren's history was a time that is now nearly obliterated by progress in almost all respects. Whether that progress is good or bad for this area remains to be seen.

When our kids were young I could permit them to run through the Brown County State Park and explore their surroundings without worrying too much about them. They could enter any house they came upon and be welcomed by those dwelling within without my having to fear a pedophile lived there. They could and did eat at the tables of everyone they knew.

In the long hot days of summer there was a shallow creek nearby where they could chase and catch little crawdads (our citified grandson had never seen them before and referred to them as baby lobsters) or minnows. It didn't matter if their old play clothes got wet and muddy or their old tennis shoes got wet. Some parts of the creek were deep enough for them to swim in for a short way so they learned to swim safely at a very young age. That environment was just a part of allowing them to grow into the fine men they have turned out to be.

In the summer's evening twilight we would often sit outside on the lawn on blankets and listen as their Dad pointed out the Big and Little Dipper, or watched for Sputnik as it traveled over our heads which made them marvel about the universe and think about space travel and how their world was changing.

Lightning bugs, or more properly fireflies I guess, lit up the evening skies and the boys had a wonderful time capturing them in their fist and placing them in a glass fruit jar. The lid had several holes punched through it for ventilation. The lights on the backsides of these bugs made the boys wonder how such things could be. No streetlights marred our views and no extraneous noise other than that provided by nature filled our world. It was a mystical, magical thrilling time. I could not have chosen a better era in which to have and rear children.

The boys spent many nights in their bedroom with the flashing of these little bugs keeping them company as I read to them while they drifted off to dreamland.

This was a much gentler time and place, probably never to be seen and enjoyed again.

So pull you up a rocking chair and place your feet on the hearth. I laid another log on the fire and turned up the reading lamp. There is a nice cup of coffee here at your right hand on that little table. Here is an afghan if you need something over your knees. If you need anything else, just let me know.

While you are reading I have a couple of chores I need to finish outside. The chickens, ducks, geese, ponies and other pets need feeding and I saw earlier that the moat around our place was now nearly filled with water. I want to release my crate of alligators and pull up the draw bridge then I'll be right back. (You will understand this after you have read the history chapter.)

In the meantime, I sure hope you enjoy meeting my friends and visiting with them in their homes in this book. Thank you for reading about them.

Helen

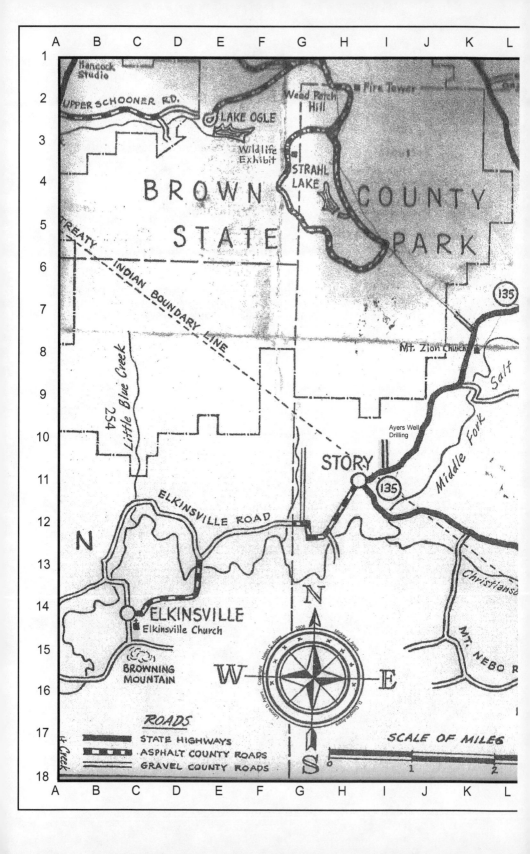

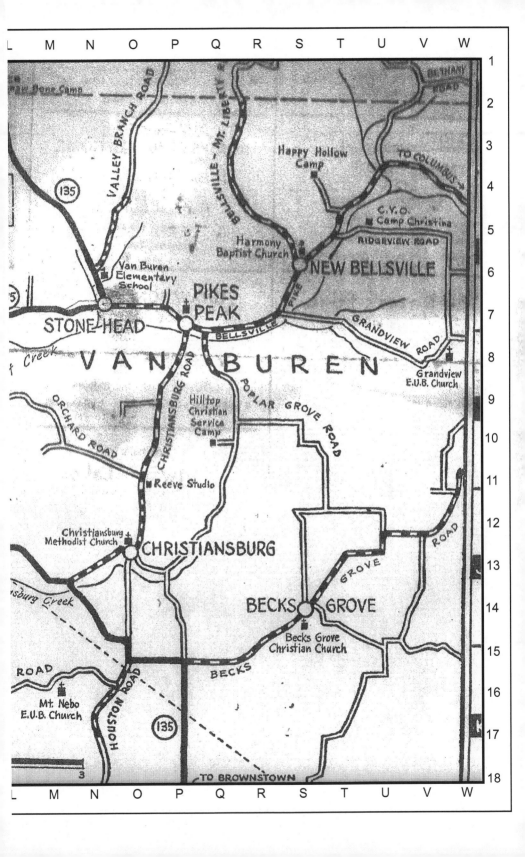

List of Homesteads

G-12	Anthony, Pauline and Bert
G-10	Aspenson, Richard and Mary
G-10	Ayers, Albert (Pink) and Eleanor
J-09	Ayers, Arnold and Myrtie
H-11	Ayers, Donald and Lenore
I-11	Ayers, Mickey and Helen
H-11	Ayers, Scott and Sandra
I-11	Ayers, Susie and Bernell
S-07	Bailey, Maxine and girls
P-07	Beauchamp, Doc
S-11	Birdsong, Joan
L-03	Blaney, Clarence
C-11	Bohall, Bob and Joe
I-12	Brand, Bud, Eva and kids
O-07	Brand, Johnny
P-14	Bredewater, George and Nancy
H-11	Carmichael, Icel and Chloe
J-10	Carmichael, Kenneth and Jewell
N-13	Carmichael, Thelma and Lee
P-07	Clark, Eleanor
S-12	Donaldson, Keith, Dorothy, Kay
G-12	Fleetwood, Bud and Louise
G-12	Fleetwood, Howard and Sharlot
SR46	Fleetwood, Chet and Maxine
O-07	Gredy, Jim
N-07	Gredy, Laurent and Grace
R-14	Harris, Mary
J-10	Hedrick, Bob and Maxine
J-10	Hedrick, Ralph and Brunell
G-12	Hedrick, Ted and Kay
G-10	Hedrick, Albert, Suz, Clothie
M-07	Henderson, Louis and Mabel
J-10	Hillenburg, Ansel
S-13	Huffman, Gary and Judy
N-07	Kritzer, Rex
L-09	Kritzer, Kenneth
C-14	Lucas, Paul and Lee Roy
N-06	Matlock, Nobel and Florence
Q-09	Moore, Aquilla and Laverne
S-07	O'Hara, Michael
S-11	Ping, Otto
H-11	Pruitt, Jim and Ann
H-11	Robertson, Toy and Clothie
L-03	Shepherd, Red and Amaryllis
Q-10	Stone, Marvin and Phyllis
N-15	Toler, Orville and Olivia
N-12	Vasquez, Jose and Chinda
O-15	Wilkerson, Amos and Olive
H-11	Wilkerson, Lizzie
G-07	Wilkerson, Jim and Radia
N-13	Wilkerson, Paul and Thelma
L-09	Williamson, Dave and Liz

Table of Contents

A History Lesson

When I married and moved to Van Buren Township in Southern Brown County, Indiana, in March 1960, it was as if time had suddenly stood still or I had suddenly moved backwards in time to a place where progress was years behind the one I had just left.

I arrived in Story in my husband's shiny new fire-engine red Chevrolet convertible, wearing my new hooded wool coat with fox-fur lining he had bought me the previous Christmas, expecting to find that things were pretty much the same as where I had been living in Jackson County.

Later that same day two furniture trucks pulled up to our little honeymoon cottage and offloaded our new furniture. This was an eye-popping event in itself. There could not have been another family in that entire area that had been able to purchase an entire house full of furniture at one time. What type of woman was I, they surely wondered if I had to have all this new furniture and I had only just gotten married? They had used the same furniture for generations.

I did not know a soul here at that time except his aunt and uncle, Amos and Olive Wilkerson so I was eager to learn about and get to know my new neighbors. I did not know it, but they were just as anxious to meet me. I had married one of their favorite sons and they wanted to look me over, perhaps to see if I deserved him I guess.

Mickey and Helen Ayers, March 6, 1960, our wedding day.

By that time in history nearly everyone had at least one car in their garage, a few had a black rotary telephone and almost everyone had a television but not many had other modern conveniences. The old crank telephones had barely been put away when I came here and nearly everyone who had a black phone was on either a four- or eight-party line. You knew the call was for your home by counting the number of long and short rings. A private number was unheard of. This was true in the Story, Indiana, community I moved to as well as the area in Jackson County where I had spent most of my childhood.

Most people in both areas had by this time stopped sleeping on corn shuck or hay-filled mattresses and had primitive, even by my standards then, mattresses on their beds. The little wimpy mattresses used by Mick's Grandma Lizzie had been made during the war years in a mattress factory which was located in Helmsburg, she told me. Quite a few were still sleeping on a feather filled mattress though. Although neither area was rich, Van Buren Township in Brown County was definitely poorer than the one I had just left.

Most folks had either found factory or construction jobs by this time so they at least had a steady, if meager, weekly income, which was a step up in the world for most of them. Judging by that standard of having a steady paycheck alone, times were beginning to improve for everyone, but there was still a long road ahead to what one could actually call prosperity.

All the time I was growing up I assumed that my family was poor. I based that assumption on the fact that we never got a lot of presents for Christmas or birthdays, and we never had a lot of cash money on hand. However, other than not having money, we had access to the most wonderful food in the world, thanks to my Mother's efforts on our farm in Jackson County and my dad's carpentry jobs in nearby towns.

We had adequate clothing and could buy shoes and coats when we needed them. If we had merely outgrown our clothing it was not discarded, but passed down the line to the next child so we, too, lived frugally. But there was no comparing my version of poor with the poor of the people I would meet when I married my husband, Mickey Ayers, and moved here. I guess being poor is a relative term at best.

Moving to Brown County at that time reminded me a great deal of the poverty we had escaped when our family left the Appalachian Mountains of Eastern Kentucky and moved to Indiana in November 1948. The plight of the residents remaining in Eastern Kentucky and those living in Van Buren Township was pretty much the same. Both areas were still gripped tightly in the fist of poverty with little hope for improvements anytime soon. This migration of the mountaineers to Indiana and other places is chronicled in my book, *Appalachian Daughter*. My personal migration to Brown County is illustrated in this book.

Living on a productive farm with able-bodied parents and eight healthy siblings meant that we could raise our own food and feed ourselves like kings. When comparing what I had given up, to what I saw when I came to Brown County, a whole new meaning of the word poor was made clear for me.

The local grocery store did not even sell cartons of milk. I called on Clothie Hedrick at the Story Store to buy a pound of bacon, a dozen eggs and a gallon of milk. She just chuckled and told me she thought her brother Lloyd might have some eggs I could buy, but she didn't know of anyone who had butchered lately. And, she said, she never had a call for milk so she didn't keep it. There went my breakfast plans. Clothie consented to order me several half-gallons each week from the dairy delivery man because I had been used to drinking milk every day from the cows on our farm.

Many of the residents of this area were still largely dependent upon wild game and fish from Salt Creek as their primary protein source. We had been growing our own protein on our farm for as long as I could remember. Looking back I could see we had been rich beyond measure at my childhood home, and my feelings of being poor now seemed ludicrous.

While my friends had been eating oleo with yellow dye mixed in it for color and shaped into neat little sticks that I thought was just so modern, we had been eating real golden creamery butter spread on home baked breads washed down with ice cold milk from our own cows, all produced on our farm.

In 1959 my very best friend all the way through high school was still sleeping on her corn shuck mattress. Geraldine's feet and her bed were heated at night by hot bricks warmed on top of a sheet iron stove during the day and wrapped in flannel rags at night to be placed in the bed. One cold winter night when I slept at her house, the wind blew some of the fragile chinking from the little logs which made up the outside bedroom walls of her home and there was freshly fallen snow piled on her floor the next morning when we woke up.

My home by then had indoor plumbing, nice windows and doors and looked like a castle compared to those of some of my childhood friends and classmates. How utterly silly children can be; we had been fabulously wealthy in comparison.

While astronauts would soon be taking a "giant leap for mankind" as they stepped foot on the surface of the moon for the first time, the people in Van Buren Township were only just beginning to take baby steps forward, but appeared to be nearly standing still. Talk about a clash between the twentieth and twenty first century!

Maybe we need to put things in better perspective by looking back even further into Brown County's history. Did the deprivation in these residents's recent past have something to do with their still slow progress by 1960? Perhaps a better understanding of that past will help us evaluate where they were in time. Let's take a look, shall we?

We were taught in school that millions of years ago when the earth was still being formed, nearly the earth's entire surface was covered with sea water. The animals that were on earth at the time were still swimming in the seas. Then great tidal waves came and went; volcanoes spewed out molten lava from the ocean's depths which would help form the outer crust of the earth and islands in the seas. Unimaginable earthquakes of humongous size were shaking and moving the plates which formed this great earth.

Drive through any mountainous area in the United States or elsewhere in the world where the rocks are easily visible and you can readily see the forces which were at once both pulling and pushing against another. I have seen this in the Black Mountain of Eastern Kentucky; the Great Smokey Mountains in Tennessee and North Carolina; and in Spain. The forces beneath the mountains pushed enormous rock layers upwards at a steep slant. That now shows clearly in the cut-throughs where today's modern roads twist through the mountains.

In Brown County, proof of the area's having once been covered with sea water can be found near Pikes Peak and Beck's Grove. Near Pike's Peak there is a hillside our sons visited several times where they could easily dig out tiny spiral shaped white seashells. These seashells were each about an inch and a quarter long, perhaps a sixteenth of an inch wide on one end and not more than an eighth of an inch across on the larger end.

Here near Beck's Grove where we now live we have found large mollusk shell fossils on our property and the prints of dozens of snake-like impressions and tiny little hoof prints in the shale rock bottom of the creek which runs behind our house. Most of these impressions have now been broken and washed further down the creek, but if someone wanted to hunt for them they could probably turn over the rocks and still find them.

One of our neighbors found what appears to be a fossilized incisor tooth from a very large prehistoric animal behind our house. If one looks closely enough, clear evidence proving prehistoric animals and sea life once existed here is abundant in this area. West of Brown County the remains of prehistoric mammoths have been found proving that once the animals left the sea and walked on land they were in this area at some time far in Brown County's past.

Then, we are told, the earth went through a few million years of a cooling off period, forming first one ice age and then millions more years later, a second ice age. As this vast layer of ice—some as much as a mile or two thick—inched its way down from the frigid north across Indiana it pushed rocks, minerals, gems and the seeds of all kinds of trees and plants before it, along with huge amounts of soil. This soil would be the building block for our present day hills here in Brown County and even farther south.

Brown County has long been the site of gold finds in the upper reaches of Salt Creek north of Gatesville. Gold panning is still promoted at the Gatesville General Store which sells sluice pans to tourists for that purpose. According to published newspaper reports, no great amount of gold was ever found, but enough was found to spark the interest of many would-be miners. The gold which has been found here was believed to have been pushed down from the north by the glaciers. As water well drillers, we have brought up bits of gold and tiny diamond like stones from the depths of the land over the years during our drilling for water.

After untold millennia this ice pack began melting. It took thousands upon thousands of years, perhaps even millions of years, to melt away completely from this area. As this ice receded it left vast reaches of rocks with a heavily over burdened layer of topsoil upon which the trees and plants we know today would one day grow and thrive.

Here in Brown County the limestone lies about 300-400 feet below the surface, yet in surrounding Bartholomew County and Monroe County, it is near the surface and easily accessible for mining. In Jackson County, to our south, they mine for river stone, gravel and sand, all totally foreign to our own county, making us unique among our neighbors.

This over burden of soil can be found around Bean Blossom and Fox's Corner in Brown County and in many other areas lying north of Brown County. My husband is a water well driller and he once drilled through a tree 105 feet below the surface at Fox's Corner. You could still see the growth rings of the tree as it was brought up from the depths, but once the pieces were exposed to the air and dried, if touched, the pieces would then become brown powder.

The son of one of our customers enjoyed playing in the mud Mickey extracted from the earth. He wasn't interested in knowing about our glacial period, he just loved the mud.

This over burden was very fine and loose in these places north of Nashville and contained vast amounts of what is termed alluvial or "old" water. There was no pump or filtration system that we knew of that could separate this loose sandy soil from the water so that water would have to be cased off and we would have to drill deeper to find potable water.

Our school books also taught us that in the process of this ice pushing its way down toward the warmer regions nearer the equator it gouged out huge rifts and holes upon the earth's surface. Other surfaces were smoothed out like it had been ironed.

These rifts and gouges became today's fresh water lakes and miles and miles of twisting rivers and smaller streams that were filled with the resultant fresh water as the ice melted. This scouring effect created the great plains of the central United States, our Great Lakes and numerous mountain ranges in both the eastern and western United States.

It is generally accepted that one of the ice ages ended its downward course across America about five miles north of Nashville near what is now known as Bean Blossom—in earlier days in our modern history it was called Georgetown. Soil Scientist, Al Donaldson believes the first ice age created the southern part of Brown County and the last one created the northern portion.

The waters from this melting ice left no rivers in our immediate area, instead leaving the rivers in the nearby counties of Bartholomew to the East and Monroe to the West. Here in Van Buren Township however, it left us many streams which we have named Salt Creek Gravel Creek, Blue Creek, Christiansburg Creek and a few others with lesser known names.

Perhaps these rivers were created in those nearby counties because the streams could not penetrate through the vast hillsides of soil the ice had pushed into this area and the waters were forced to go around the hills instead. I am no scientist so I cannot say for sure, but if one looks at a map, it appears to be so. Water will always seek its own level and way around obstacles and the surface water in Indiana flows toward the southwest into the Ohio River.

The glacier also left behind the hills which would stretch from Bean Blossom to near the Ohio River in a sort of meandering course which would make up what scholars now call the Hoosier Uplands. These forested hills would eventually be the basis for the establishment of the Hoosier National Forest.

According to the naturalists at the Brown County State Park, the tallest of these hills would actually be located about the middle of what would become in the late nineteen twenties, the Brown County State Park. This promontory is called Weed Patch Hill and though most people think it is the tallest spot in Indiana, the naturalists say it is actually the second tallest by a few feet. But, they say, if one added in the height of the old fire tower located at the top of Weed Patch Hill, it would then be the tallest peak in Indiana.

When Brown County was carved from the surrounding counties in 1836, Van Buren Township was delineated roughly on the North by the Seelmaer Hill which was a couple of miles south of State Road 46 on State Road 135 and the upper reaches of Jackson County to the South; Bartholomew County to the East and about to Gravel Creek to the West. Velma Seitz of Pike's Peak was a Seelmaer and the hill was named for her family.

Nowadays with most of Johnson Township, which was located west of Gravel Creek and bounded by Monroe County to its west and the same upper and lower reaches as Van Buren, under the waters of the Monroe Reservoir, everything south of Seelmaer Hill and lying east of the waters of Lake Monroe is now called Van Buren Township. While Van Buren Township expanded, Johnson Township just no longer existed.

Velma Seelmaer Seitz

This portion of Brown County which became Van Buren Township was more heavily wooded, steeper, hillier and less populated than any other part of the county or state. In fact, the hills were so steep and the roads were so bad for so many years, that Van Buren Township was almost a step-child to the rest of Brown County. It was almost inaccessible for many years. It was only after State Road 135 was well established as a paved highway that the area could readily be accessed by all; while all the land lying from Bean Blossom north, clear into Canada, was flat as a pancake due to the great glaciers.

For a long time in the county's early history, if you were unable to pay your property taxes, you could work off an equal amount to pay them by working on the roads in your area. That is how a goodly number of the roads were improved. The men would take their horses or mules into the creeks pulling what was known as a slip scoop and harvest the gravel from the creek. This gravel would then be shoveled upon the nearby roads.

One notable taxpayer and tombstone carver in the Van Buren area by the name of Henry Cross paid his taxes by carving a man's head on a chunk of limestone and inscribing the names of and directions to several other towns. The statue he carved now marks the location of Stone Head. The directional sign has been the target of college age exploits over the years. The college students have removed it two or three times but it has always been found and returned to its resting place. It has been used as a hat rack in a college dorm and as a directional sign post in other towns. But it is addicted to Van Buren and always returns to its normal home.

The Stone Head marker was carved by Henry Cross to pay his taxes.

Van Buren would be populated by very sturdy immigrants from the Carolinas on the eastern coastal United States. Still others came here from Tennessee and Kentucky and from areas of Ohio. These early settlers to Brown County arrived in Elkinsville and Schooner Valley just west of Nashville long before Brown County actually became a county. A few Indians still roamed this area when these early settlers arrived and a few of today's families, my husband's included, can claim Indians in their ancestry. The Ten O'clock Line Treaty marked the end of the Indians in this area. An historic marker stands at Story that depicts the saga of this treaty.

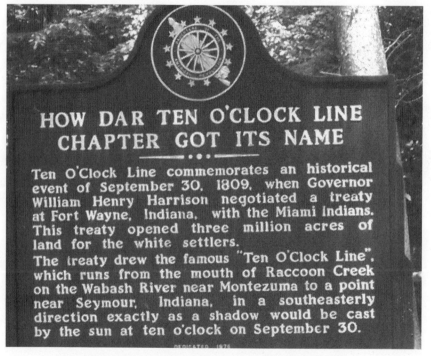

The Ten O'Clock Line Treaty marker stands today in
Story to mark the end of the Indians in this area.

These early settlers stayed in this area primarily because it was similar to the regions they had just left. The hills and hollers and almost total isolation reminded them of the homes they had left and they remembered how to survive in that type of environment. They found a very narrow valley running between the hillsides from Elkinsville to east of Story a few miles. Once you reach Bartholomew County to the east, this valley opens out into vast stretches of farmland and the hillsides disappear entirely.

Most of these early settlers built their homes in this valley but placed them slightly higher upon the hillsides to avoid the dangers of Salt Creek in flood stage. In this valley and alongside this creek they also dug a salt well at Elkinsville which product they traded for necessities. This is how the name for Salt Creek originated. Another salt well was located at Stone Head. There are other areas in Brown County where salty water can be found when drilling a water well. Those areas include Axsom Branch and Trevlac (which is Calvert spelled backward to honor its earliest settler) among others.

The area's early male settlers were trappers and fur traders; and, they grew their own vegetables and enough domestic animals to provide meat and milk for their families. To obtain pork meat sometimes meant they had to go into the hills and drive out and kill a wild pig that had fattened on the mast of the forest. They also hunted squirrels, rabbits, wild turkeys and several species of waterfowl, and in later years white tailed deer, to be used as meat on their tables. In harsh times they ate less desirable animals but avoided eating these animals when they had plenty. It was rare that they ever butchered a beef animal, probably because they were so rare and so valuable to add to their herds.

George Bredewater's rendition of a ring neck pheasant
which once roamed the hills and valleys of Van Buren
Township. It is rare to see one of these birds today.

Salt Creek abundantly provided the early settlers with plenty of fish that could be eaten fresh or salted down and placed in wooden barrels they had made for this purpose so the fish could be used at a later time when the water might have been frozen over with ice for example. Times for them were indeed rough, but these were roughly grown men and women. They knew how to survive on almost anything or, alternatively, on almost nothing.

The Great Depression had been and gone nearly a quarter century prior to my arrival here leaving the sturdy people in Van Buren Township hardly any the wiser. They had been so poor before being told they were in a depression, they really hardly knew it had happened.

Never wealthy enough to hold securities and bonds, and with not even enough money to open a bank account, what did most of them have to lose materially? They already bartered with the peddler men for the groceries they needed so money held little luster for them. Their dignity and self esteem was lost amid the want of the hardest times ever known in our great country. The most important things left to them were their families and their belief in God.

If you ever get the chance to view some of the old family pictures of this time and this place, 1930 to about 1960, pay particular attention to the faces, hairdos and clothing of these residents. It is almost a certainty you will see no smiles on their faces; even the group pictures of school children are nearly devoid of smiles. Many of the children were sent to school bare footed because they had no shoes. The rigors of deprivation and hard work in their life are reflected in the faces of those photographed.

Otto Ping of Pikes Peak captured the hard-hitting images of the early times in Van Buren. Mr. Ping tried many avenues to earn a living, but failed miserably at most of them. However, he was a talented photographer and was able to record the history of this area in graphic photos which might have been lost had the negatives and glass plates not been found in his home's attic. None of his pictures were termed "artistic" but instead they recorded a time and place in our history that would have been lost without his photographs.

Otto Ping and his wife Clara in their twilight years.

Those photos and plates were donated in their entirety to the Indiana Historical Society. Please refer to a book the society published about this noted resident in 1994 titled *"Otto Ping 1900-1940."* The book shows many of his gripping photographs and it has several scholarly notations throughout the book of his life here in Van Buren. He would live until 1975 and be 92 years old when he died but he stopped his itinerant photography business about 1940 because by then cameras were inexpensive enough that most people could buy at least a Brownie camera and take their own family photographs, that book tells us.

Examine the quality of their clothing in some of these old photos. Most of it was hand sewn by the women and looked it. Some of these sad-eyed stern-faced women had actually woven the cloth on their homemade looms, dyed the material with plants or nuts they had gathered from the nearby woods, and assembled the pieces by hand to make these sorry looking garments.

The clothing they wore may have kept in the body's heat and covered their nakedness, but it surely had not much to do with fashion. But I don't believe fashion was what these hard-working women were hoping to achieve. They were doing the very best they knew how to do to clothe their husbands, themselves and their many children as best they could in whatever way they could. And there sure was not very much for them to smile about. The simple act of daily living was very, very difficult and it took every ounce of their energy just to face each new day.

Some women could not hack the job so they just laid down and died, leaving those behind to fend for themselves the best they could. These tired, work-worn women did not have the strength or heart remaining to care enough to live, so they gave their families into God's capable hands and went to their rest.

The depression had no more than passed them by when WWII came along and sugar and other grocery necessities, gasoline, oil, tires and automobiles became even scarcer. The qualifying families were issued ration stamps for the bare necessities but they still had to continually "make do." The news they heard on their battery operated radios, which they used for only short periods each day to learn the war news of their men fighting "over there," kept them in a perpetual state of anxiety. Electricity would not come to this area until two or three years after the war ended.

You must understand that these people were from a very secluded area and environment. They believed most of what was told to them by the newscasters of the day, especially Lowell Thomas and President Franklin D. Roosevelt himself, when they had enough "juice" to run their radios. At night they extinguished their lights early to prevent becoming targets of bombs—I'm serious here—some in this area really did this.

The soldiers from Camp Atterbury occasionally marched through Story to bivouacs further west, but I don't know that Story, Indiana, was ever a target for bombs. My husband says these soldiers ran over his tricycle with one of their vehicles. He is convinced to this day that they did this on purpose.

RETURN THIS SLIP WHEN MAKING PAYMENT

..............*Van Buren*..............Township
Brown County, Indiana

Duplicate Number ....

Date .... 19 ....

Lizzie Wilkeson

May Tax	...........8.	...6.5
November Tax	....	....
Delinquent Tax	....	....
TOTAL TAX	....	....

If the first installment is not paid by the first Monday in May, eight per cent will be added.

If the first installment is paid by the first Monday in May and the second installment is not paid by the first Monday in November eight per cent is added to the second instalment. Five per cent will be added yearly for all Delinquent Tax over one year old.

In remittances I prefer Checks, drafts or American Express Money Order.

When making payment please send self addressed envelope.

Treasurer Brown County

Grandma Lizzie's tax bill for half a year was
only $8.65 on this undated receipt.

A trip to Nashville to pay their taxes twice each year or a trip to Columbus for some necessity or another was a trip of unbelievable proportions. The trips had to be carefully planned. Today in little more than an hour, you can easily make either of these trips from anywhere in Van Buren Township and return, but in these earlier times in a horse and buggy on the muddy and horribly rutted roads, this might have been a two-day trip with a stay under the stars somewhere overnight.

If you lived at Story for example, a simple trip to hear a preacher give his sermon in nearby Elkinsville or Pike's Peak, each just a few miles away, had to be thought out and planned in advance because these trips meant walking a goodly ways from home and would take several hours if not most of the day to accomplish.

To aid the war effort and do their part to help their men who were serving in the Army, those remaining at home joined the patriotic throng who collected scrap metals to make bullets. There was no such thing as throwing away a piece of metal of any sort; every scrap was saved and turned in, even food tins. A metal cooking pot that sprung a leak was mended over and over if necessary by the tinker man and would never be simply discarded.

And, they saved and turned in all the old grease they could dispense with to make glycerin for coating those bullets their men were firing on the front lines. The local newspaper, *The Brown County Democrat,* ran weekly reports on how much was conserved each week by local residents for the war effort.

Reading these newspaper accounts of the war years is fascinating reading. I spent days and weeks pouring over them when I had nothing else to do. These families took their responsibilities very seriously and they passed their fears of bombings and invasions along to their children which would affect them too for the next few years.

By the time the war began the women in this area had already adapted about as much as they could adapt to the hard times. There just was nothing left in their lives that could be cut back on any further and still allow them to exist. Only a relative few owned cars, so gasoline rationing meant little to them, other than the fact they might be able to trade their gas and tire ration stamps for some other necessity they did need.

Shoes were scarce, but the ones they had could be mended, re-soled, re-heeled, toe and heel taps applied, and if out-grown, could be passed down to the next youngest for a long time. Those too poor to repair their shoes placed cardboard inside them to cover the holes that had worn through the soles. Things that once had been knitted were disassembled and other things such as socks and caps were newly made from the same old yarn.

Judging from the number of shoe lasts that are found in home auctions today, nearly every home must have had one of these contraptions for making or mending shoes. Perhaps along with maintaining the outside chores, it would have fallen to the men of the household to be shoe cobblers. Some probably even killed and skinned the animals and tanned the hides themselves to make the family's shoes since nearly all of the men were very highly skilled woodsmen.

When making coffee, the women spooned the ground coffee beans into a pot of water each morning and kept adding water all day, pushing the pot to a back burner on the wood-burning cookstove to boil every iota of taste they could extract from the crushed coffee beans—that is if they were fortunate enough to have honest to goodness coffee beans. The residue would finally be thrown into the chicken pens for them to peck at and sort through.

Actual coffee beans were scarcer than hen's teeth during the Great Depression and the war years. If they actually bought coffee beans at all they chose the very cheapest brand they could find, usually a store brand such as A & P and ground it in their own hand cranked coffee grinders at home. Some stores charged a penny or two per pound to grind the beans for them, so most families had their own coffee grinder.

By this time in the deeply depressed economy, these resourceful women used other sources of flavorings to mimic coffee. Some parched shelled corn, then crushed the corn, using that as a substitute for coffee. Others grew or bought chicory. Newspapers and magazines gave ideas for this type of making do. A few depended upon the red sassafras roots they harvested from the nearby woods to give meaning to their morning cup.

Still others depended upon this same sassafras root, tied into small "hands," to provide them with a steady income when it was sold to the root buyers or huckster peddlers. The pay was small, but if all the members of a family worked together to tie the hands then some money could be realized.

The sassafras roots would be dug up along fence rows or other untended places, cleaned well and the bark removed. Then using a sharp knife, small strips about three inches long could be slivered from the remaining root and when bound together, made up a handful or "hand" of the pungent root.

Sassafras was a quickly renewable resource and for many years was harvested and sold by poor families of this area in this manner. For many families these hands of sassafras roots, and the dried bounty of other roots such as golden seal, blood root, may apple root and ginseng they scoured from the nearby woods, became their primary source of income.

The boys and men depended upon the trapping of wild animals to provide some more much needed money. They trapped raccoons, minks, foxes, beavers and muskrats in and around Salt Creek. Even as late as 1959 a bounty of $3 was paid if you turned in a pair of fox ears to the county treasurer so every fox caught or found dead would be scalped. When the skins of these animals had been stretched, defatted and dried they would be sold to fur buyers. These skins, from earlier times through the present day, were very valuable commodities.

Many of the menfolk in this area, some over 40-years-old and having several children, were inducted into the Army during WW II, pushing the women into ever more dire straits.

Trapper Oscar Ayers shows the furs he trapped during one cold winter.

The women whose husbands were away at war now not only had their normal chores of growing a garden and preserving the produce and minding the children as they always had had to do, it was now their responsibility also to mend fences and structures, go to work in the fields, look after and tend any livestock and some went to work in factories. Older children helped in these chores but it fell to the woman of the house to make sure the chores were completed. Each day brought new challenges to these struggling families. It was either do that or do without many of life's basic necessities.

Even if they had raised enough vegetables in their garden and preserved them for later use to feed the children and themselves in the coming cold months, their horse, mule, cow, chickens and maybe a pig if they were lucky enough to have any animals at all—and some did not have any—also had to be provided for.

The work was a never ending proposition beginning sometimes before daylight each day and lasting into the night. Every child able to walk would have been enlisted to help with these chores. Only the infants of the household would have been spared work of some sort or another. Even a very small child could gather eggs or carry in kindling and other little chores so every member of the household pitched in to help their mothers.

It did the women no good at all to complain about their plight; there was no one in their neighborhood that was not in the same boat they were. Maybe if a neighbor had an older son, he might be asked to help a lone woman do a few of her heavy chores, but most of the time, with so many of their men gone to war, all the chores fell to these women and children.

During the Great Depression and World War II, several of the residents of southern Brown County were forced to give one or more of their children away for adoption. It was either do that or allow them to starve, so with sorrow in their hearts they gave their little ones to strangers or sometimes to relatives to be reared.

Usually these women gave away their youngest, most needy child. The older children could help in the gardens and fields to help support the remaining family members. These were some very tough decisions and they were not made lightly by either the giver or the taker of the children. The children would never be forgotten, but their names might rarely be spoken because of the pain it would permit to enter the mother's heart.

A few of these children, middle-aged when I met them, who had been given away by their mothers, stopped by the *Brown County Democrat* while I worked there from 1972 to 1993 to look up stories about, or to inquire about, their birth families. It had been a dreadfully sad time for everyone. Often times I would know their birth families and could help them locate someone who had personal knowledge to pass on of their family's whereabouts. Some of them I could not help because I did not know their birth parents or none of their family still lived locally. But when I could help one, I did so.

Also during these same years many whole families had to leave Brown County to earn a living elsewhere. Several families traveled to the fertile farmlands of Illinois and became sharecroppers or merely farm hands to ensure that their families had enough to eat and could survive the rigors of the times. Some of these families would never return to Brown County to live, but a few did, notably in the Story area, the Howard and Sharlot Fleetwood family.

Sharlot's parents had fallen on very hard times and were in danger of losing their home. Her parents, Isom and Sally Arwine Wilkerson, begged Sharlot and her husband Howard to return to Brown County and take over the family farm, and they did return to help out and stayed here the rest of their lives. Others stayed in Illinois permanently. This was told to me by Maxine Fleetwood who married Chester Fleetwood, one of Sharlot and Howard's sons.

Electricity was strung from pole to pole through this rural area in late 1947. This electrification of rural areas made things marginally better for these residents, but not enough to make a huge difference for some time. Most residents still had to rely on their battery operated radios on a limited basis each day to hear the news and weather reports. Had they hooked on to the rural electric it would have meant a monthly bill, and no matter how small it was, if they had no steady income, then most could not afford even that little bit of luxury or debt.

Howard and Sharlot Fleetwood.

By 1960 only a few homes in this area had telephones but most had televisions to lighten their days. However, most of them could tune in only one or two channels; one from Indianapolis and one from Louisville. Several still depended upon kerosene lanterns and lamps for illumination and did not even own a television. The more modern inventions would not appear on the scene until some years later.

Fear was a living factor for some, fear of what exactly I am not sure about. Perhaps they feared the future and the changes the future might bring for them, or maybe they were afraid another disaster they had no control over would strike them, but some remained scared even as late as the mid 1950s. Maybe, remembering their recent past, they were just waiting for the other shoe to drop. The past had not treated them gently that is for sure. At any rate, they remained fearful and didn't care if that fear showed.

Some very tumultuous years were only just very recently behind them. They were afraid to spend much money and would go into debt only to purchase an automobile to provide transportation in order for them to work elsewhere. They did not want to make waves or cause other people to notice them. This was truly an amazing place at that time in history.

Family old timers tell the story of one elderly widow woman in the area who kept something plugged into every electrical outlet in the house. Once someone asked her why she did that and she responded she didn't want the "juice," as electricity was referred to at that time, to leak out and cost her more money.

There probably would not have been more than two or three outlets for lights and plug-ins in the entire house and almost without exception, these receptacles would hang from a long piece of the electric wire left suspended from the ceiling. Usually there was a socket attached to the wire that permitted you to screw in a light bulb that still needed an on/off crank switch to make it work; or, you could remove the bulb and screw in an adapter that allowed you to plug in an iron or a toaster or other small appliance of some sort. The wiring of their houses for electricity was rudimentary at best.

Even as late as 1960, the people of this area still depended upon split wood and/or coal for heating their homes and cooking; a well for drawing or pumping their drinking water; they had no indoor plumbing and would not see that until the 1970's.

Doctors were by then non-existent in the small towns like Story. However, Story, Bellsville and nearby Houston in Jackson County had all had doctors at one time, but they had long since gone to larger towns to practice their skills or had died. Those men were Drs. Story, Ralphy and Cummings. Dr. Cummings was our family doctor down in Jackson County for many years and he plied his trade until he was well into his 80s, first in Houston and later in Ewing.

The residents recalled that well into the 1900's some of the country doctors were still practicing dual careers; they cared for both animals and humans. Sanitary procedures were nearly non-existent here as they were in many other places and the doctors, for the most part, were more dangerous to your health than the illness or injury for which he had been called in would have been.

These earlier doctors would often attend a sick cow or horse in the farmer's barn, then go inside the home and assist at the birth of a baby or tend to a human illness without stopping along the way to wash and sterilize either his instruments or his hands. This was very common and it would not be until sometime in the 1940s that most doctors began learning to practice better personal hygiene between patients.

All that remains today of old Doc Story's office in Story.

George Bredewater shows how some of the old-time doctors
probably traveled to see their patients. I believe the drawing is
of Otto Ping on the muddy state road just north of Stone Head,
but most of the doctors had conveyances like this one.

It was this kind of almost arrogant disregard for their patient's welfare, in the first half of the twentieth century and before, that caused so many women to die in childbirth of childbed fever. It also left many men the job of finding another, often younger woman to marry and care for his children and tend his home. It was not uncommon for these men to marry three or four times and have children with each wife. These men and women were not knowledgeable about birth control so babies were continually being born to women whose bodies were already worn out from giving birth every year or two and tending to all their chores at the same time. The constant drain of childbirth on the women's physical resources was great and many of them died.

For various reasons these women, for the most part spinsters, who became replacement wives and stepmothers had never expected to marry. Some of them had chosen to stay at home to care for their elderly parents, or had finished raising their brothers and sisters if their parents had died. Some were just homely enough they did not expect to ever attract a man. They would jump at the chance to marry a man even if he had several children. Doing so would put them in that elite, smug group of women who had a man of their own.

Her husband may have been uglier than a mud fence or even mean to her, but he was a male, therefore someone to be desired. The marriage might or might not have contained love but other factors made up for that lack if it didn't and these women were content with their roles. They could now stand apart from their wallflower sisterhood and alongside their new-found married kinswomen and smugly talk about their husband and children, or how much work they had to do, etc. But you can bet they loved rubbing it in to their former group of friends that they now had a man of their own and their lives were now worth much more than it had been.

In nearly every family there would be an older woman, sometimes referred to as a "granny woman," who acted as doctor and midwife to the rest of the family. This woman could sew up cuts, set broken bones, bring down fevers or birth babies. They had effective cures for many common ailments. Only the most catastrophic wound or illness would cause a real doctor to be called in. Appendicitis, now almost commonly an in and out hospital procedure, was often fatal. The same could be said for influenza, measles and other childhood diseases; worldwide pandemics of these diseases alone caused millions of people to die.

The graveyards in Van Buren are populated by people whose lives were cut short by these common everyday illnesses which are now easily avoided through childhood immunization. If you were operated on successfully by a doctor for appendicitis, you still sometimes died for lack of sanitation by the doctor.

The advent of the common aspirin was such a gigantic leap forward in medicine that it would be hailed as a miracle pill. Now the granny women had something besides willow bark tea for the worst pain. Recent research shows the lowly aspirin tablet is also a great advance in the fight against heart attack and stroke and half of today's population is now advised to use aspirin every day to prevent these afflictions.

Then penicillin came along and the women had a medicine that could potentially bring a loved one back from the brink of death.

These two medicines probably made as much difference in the daily lives of these women as anything that had been developed for the medical field prior to that time. They were cheap enough nearly everyone could afford them and they were superbly effective.

Similar to the granny woman, there was likewise a woman or two in most families—or who at least lived in the neighborhood—that assisted the dying in doing so. They further served their patients after death by preparing their bodies for burial. Most times these women worked right alongside their sister granny women so they would have been on the spot if the patient died. I'm not sure they had a specific name like granny woman who cared for the living, but their services were invaluable both to the deceased and to the survivors.

This very special woman would sit with the sick for days or hours as needed and tempt their patient to eat bits of food they thought would be good for them; they sang hymns and offered prayers; comforted the children and spoke words of solace to the spouse. When the one dying finally took that final breath, this woman would then bathe the body, dress it and make it ready to be placed in a homemade pine board casket. She would prepare, or cause to be prepared, a great feast which would be enjoyed by everyone after they attended the funeral. Food and words of comfort was what she offered the survivors and medicine was what the granny women offered the suffering.

If the deceased was a woman who had died in childbirth, the baby, if it also died, would most generally have been buried enfolded in its mother's arms. If it was the baby who died and the mother who survived, these special women would tenderly bathe the baby and place it in the family dress reserved for babies; then it would be swaddled in a blanket and placed in the mother's arms.

If this special woman was a really good one, the mother might be permitted to hold her child as long as she needed to form that special bond between mother and child. When the mother was ready to see them, the husband and other children would be admitted to her bedroom and they too could touch and see and talk about the baby and maybe give it a name before it was buried.

The parents would be encouraged to count this dead child among their own and would be handed the family bible in which they could record its birth, name, and date of death. All bibles of this time had pages reserved for recording this type of historical family information. I have read recently where this practice of parent/dead child bonding is now being promoted again. It was a good idea then as well as now.

Some of these special women, like some of the doctors of that time period, were not this nice and would permit the mother only a brief glance if that at the child she had carried for nine months beneath her breast. The husband and older children might not even be allowed to see or touch it. Instead she might wrap the dead baby in a blanket and tell the father to see to its burial. But, like the doctors, there were good ones and bad ones.

In my husband's family the granny woman was his maternal grandma, Lizzie Wilkerson. These wise women were often times far more careful of their handling of the sick than the doctors of the times were, but occasionally the real doctors would have a medication these talented women did not have which could mean the difference between life and death to their loved one, so when all else failed, a doctor would be called in to assist.

Lizzie Wilkerson,
used many effective if
unorthodox cures.

Thelma Wilkerson,
a friend to the
Granny Woman.

The woman who attended our dead and dying, without actually being named as such, was Thelma Wilkerson. She was also the cook at the Van Buren Elementary School for many years and the children loved her. Outside of my mother, she was the best cook I ever knew. I don't recall many people in the neighborhood dying without Thelma quietly offering to sit with them, or say a prayer or sing for them, or offer her cooking talents or those of others of her church for the post funeral meal.

I had been deathly sick in 1993 and doctors did not think I would survive but I lived to surprise both them and myself. It was after I came home to recuperate that I entered a creative period of time in which I was able to write many songs and poetry.

Once when I was working on my computer I kept seeing a file that said simply, "Thelma." I ignored it several times but finally was curious enough to open the file and there was the neatest poem I had written about Thelma that I did not even remember writing, but it had my name and the date I had written it on the page. It was so nice I copied it and sent copies of it to her children.

Thelma Tabor Wilkerson with her husband of 64 years, Paul.

By the time I knew Thelma most funerals were routinely being held at the Bond Funeral Home in Nashville so I don't know that she ever served in the fuller capacity of assisting the dying. She sat with my mother-in-law, Lenore Ayers, many times as she lay dying of cancer, but that could have been because they both belonged to the

Christiansburg Church and had been friends their entire lives. After
Lenore was buried we returned home to a sagging table of delicious
food, all thanks to Thelma and her church sisters.

Thelma

Seems like there's always one like her in our neighborhood,
A woman of stature who wants to do good.
She's there when you need her, you have only to call,
And she will come running spring, summer or fall.

She knows how to do most everything,
From birthing babies to holding hymn sings.
She's laid out the dying, taken food to the ill,
Given good advice, but left nary a bill.

For many years she helped out at school,
Feeding our children, she worked like a mule.
Many kind words she's given, many knees has she kissed,
When she retired, she surely was missed.

Our kids called her "Felma" as they told me each day,
Of the good things she baked, and those she hugged on the way.
Now both grown men with kids of their own,
They still ask about Felma when they come home.

Now Thelma is getting up there in years,
Some sickness she's had, and she's shed many tears.
For those that she loved and sent on to their rest,
Thelma, my neighbor, we've surely been blessed.

Happy birthday to you, I would wish many more for thee,
If they could be lived both in health and harmony.
So today I'll just say Happy Birthday, my friend,
Blessed be the days from here to the end.

Written and Copyrighted by Helen Ayers May 23, 1999

Thelma loved children. I think she would be very happy today if she could know that her granddaughter Amanda Wheeler Austin and husband Trent Austin are the parents of four babies between 7 months and two years. Of course, three of those babies are triplets, two girls and one boy and the one older boy. They are living in and renovating the homestead that Thelma and Paul once owned. It takes grandma Loretta Wheeler and several others to help provide Amanda a support system to care for the babies but they are so fat and cheerful and growing like little weeds. I really think Thelma would be busting buttons off her clothing she would be so proud of them. And, you would have to muzzle her to stop her bragging about these adorable babies.

Mickey's grandpa, Grover Wilkerson, died in 1958. At that time funerals were still being held in the deceased's homes so the ritual of holding funerals in the funeral homes arrived after that time for many families in this area.

The Bond Funeral Home placed a number of cardboard fans in your home or the church or in their own facility to be used during a funeral service in warm weather. Usually the fans would show a religious scene on one side or have the name of the funeral home on it for advertising purposes. Each fan had a short wooden handle for ease in wielding it. I am including a picture of one of these fans, probably from the late forties or early 1950s. The pictures on this particular fan show a much younger and much thinner Jack and Earl Bond than the ones I knew. Both are now dead and their funeral home has been sold to others.

*Bond Funeral Home advertising fan. Notice that it could
be reached by dialing only two numbers, 4-0.*

Notice that the phone number for the funeral parlor included only two digits, the numbers 4-0. When I moved here in 1960 telephones were numbered LO8 (for Locust) or whatever plus four numbers, therefore the 4-0 for the funeral home was much older.

WWII was barely over and the men returned home when suddenly some of the men were again conscripted to serve in the Korean War. Many still had not yet had time to get their families completely reestablished and their home and barn maintenance chores caught up before they were gone again for several more years.

Some of these men left children and pregnant wives behind once again. It seemed they were away for many years, leaving the women and the children to more or less fend for themselves. Most would send military "allotments" back home to their wives, but this sometimes was no more than $20 a month, but every little bit helped against the ever constant threat of hunger. Most of the women remaining behind would have foregone the $20 monthly check if they could have had their husband back home working alongside them.

It would take these women and their men, once they returned from Korea, many years working at a steady pace, to put their farms and homesteads back together again and be able to provide a slightly better standard of living for their families.

There were few vehicles in the area during the 1930s to mid 1950s so the residents depended upon huckster wagons for many of those years to bring groceries to them. There was a Monday Peddler and a Thursday Peddler who came every week to Story and other small towns bringing necessities to these little homesteads. One peddler was a Mr. Hamblen and the other was Mr. McDonald of Bean Blossom, but I don't know which day each of them came.

*Remnants of an old huckster wagon were found
on Blue Creek Road at the Bohall place.*

The hucksters might trade a bag of flour to a woman in Story in exchange for three or four dozen of her chicken eggs. Then further down the road, a woman might have needed a dozen eggs. She, in turn, might exchange a peck of sweet potatoes or a live goose, duck or a roasting chicken for the eggs.

By the time the peddler returned to his place of beginning, his wagons were just as full as when he began his tour, but it now contained different produce and fowl. If he lived in Nashville or Bean Blossom, he could sell those country fresh items to the people living in the more urban setting. There were buyers for all his wares. Actual cash money was nearly non-existent; bartering for goods was the norm.

George Bredewater created this drawing of the Hamblen family's huckster wagon. It visited from house to house one day each week.

Kay Hedrick found this old photo of the C. H. McDonald huckster wagon in her family photo album.

During the war years it was common for the men and women of this area to hitch a ride into Columbus occasionally to purchase some essential item such as lard, for example, for their homes that could not be obtained from the peddler men or raised on their own homesteads. Sometime, I have been told, there were so many Brown Countians standing on the corner of Third and Washington Streets waiting for a ride home, that the locals there nicknamed the corner, Brown County Corner.

There was a Carmichael's Fish Sandwich Shop, located on Jackson Street I believe, in Columbus. It would be from this fish shop that the women would buy used fish grease to use in their home cooking. The grease would already have been used over and over again by this fish shop prior to their selling it to these country women. The women though, grateful to obtain anything during the war years, would use this fish grease as lard in their cooking and it was a crucial ingredient when making lye soap for bathing and washing the family's clothing. My husband remembers as a little boy that everything they ate that had been fried, tasted of fish.

Many of the local residents had seen their property taken by the State of Indiana by virtue of imminent domain in the late 1920's to establish the Brown County State Park, Indiana's largest state park At one time the entire 15,000 plus acres, which now constitute the park, was privately owned, much of it by Van Buren Township residents..

If you walk the old park trails today you will still occasionally come upon abandoned home sites. These trails were originally scoured into the landscape by the feet of earlier settlers of this area. Those early settlers followed game trails which later become Indian trails which even later had become their own trails from one community to another. The trails ran along the ridge tops so walking was easier. Many of Brown County's roads would follow these same trails when its highway system originated explaining why our roads are so up and down and twist from side to side.

You will know you have found an old home site because one can usually see the corner and foundation stones which held up the homes; the old roofless cellars, once walled up with native stone but now with doors ajar or missing completely or maybe today it is just a bare hole in the ground; and perhaps you will see an uncovered dug well. It pays to watch where you step if you get off the beaten trails inside the park. Generally too, you will find an old apple, pear or peach tree—perhaps one still bearing some stunted fruit—along with a few flowering bulbs or other shrubs that once graced this home site.

These people did not want to move elsewhere but they were given no option by the state authorities. Their land was taken by the State of Indiana; money for which was placed in a bank in Nashville in their name; and they were told to abandon the property because their home was going to be torn or burned down to make way for a state park.

Bewildered and afraid of those in authority, many of these residents had already relocated prior to the worst days of the Great Depression. As it would turn out, they would be but the first of several groups who gave up their homes in Van Buren Township to benefit another group of people.

It is nice for the present day and future generations to have the expanse of this great park preserved for the public's use, but for the people whose lands were wrested from them so forcefully and ruthlessly, it was disgraceful. Today the scabs and scars of this forced removal have healed, but those who are yet able to remember this part of the past have not forgotten.

Then another more sobering event was taking shape that would see many dozens more families fleeing before the bulldozers arrived; being forcefully removed from this same little area. This time it was because the nearby city of Bloomington needed a more adequate water supply and others wanted a water recreational area. Again, people in Van Buren and Johnson Township to the west would be chosen for removal.

The Army Corps of Engineers was mapping the area, buying up homesteads so the Monroe Reservoir could be built and telling the people to move. Again, if they objected, the money was deposited in a bank in Nashville in their name and bulldozers were dispatched to demolish the homes. Some bridges near Elkinsville were destroyed to prevent re-entry into the area.

This project began in the late 1950's with the mapping and surveying of the area and by 1964 it was an accomplished fact. The towns of Youno and Elkinsville, among others, were obliterated from local county maps and very few people were left in the western part of southern Brown County. In fact, one whole township, Johnson, was gobbled up for this latest project. The few remaining residents on the eastern shore of the reservoir became part of Van Buren Township's population. Those on the western shore of the reservoir were made a part of Washington Township.

Many residents did not know why their acreage was spared and their neighbor's property bought in this takeover. Maybe it was because of the capricious method of mapping and buying by the

Corps, that some homesteads or some part of them was spared. In later years, these few remaining homesteads would again be home for some residents.

The reservoir project would also remove the only access road directly west from Story to Bloomington, forcing anyone driving to Bloomington from Story to make the far longer trip around through Stone Head and Nashville. Not long after the Monroe Reservoir filled with water, the roads leading west went underwater and remain under today.

The other sad part about all these people being moved out and the area flooded with water is that you cannot access the reservoir from any point in Van Buren Township. You must first drive miles away to enjoy this giant body of water. Those in authority took and took until nothing much was left worth taking, but they made no provision for the remaining residents in this area to enjoy what they had created.

The earlier settlers of Elkinsville and Youno were basically from Ohio, Tennessee, Kentucky and the Carolinas. They had moved to Brown County in the early 1800s, years before Brown County was actually formed and officially named in 1836.

Patriotic, many of them served their country in times of war. During the Civil War there were many of the Elkins family men, for whom Elkinsville was named, who served in the war. The records of this war that I reviewed do not indicate whether they all came from the same household.

Then by 1964, almost everyone in this area was gone.

Still other people were removed from this area to make way for the Yellowwood State Forest, the Hoosier National Forest and the

Charles Deem Wilderness Area. Eventually the population of Van Buren Township dwindled until only a few hundred people lived in its vastness.

My children would later tell me that living in Van Buren Township meant it was like I was living in a little cocoon; or like being on an island surrounded by water that just needed alligators added to the water to keep progress out. I love their analogies.

They said this to me after they were grown and each had traveled this big world on business pursuits; seeing that not everyone could live as we were living in this beautiful area.

I was always one who never liked to watch the news on television; I wanted the weather to surprise me each day; my local newspaper was a weekly one; and I rarely traveled very far from home. Even riddled with poverty Van Buren Township was, and still is, a beautiful area. I am content to live here among my many friends on our "island."

Van Buren is now making a comeback, but it is not one that most people who have lived here a long time want to see. We have become accustomed to living on our "island," even snug in a cocoon, and do not want to be disturbed. But more and more often, people from the cities are discovering the joys of living in this almost sylvan area and are buying up the property that is for sale, paying exorbitant prices for the right to live here, and building enormous homes.

There are three children's summer camps located here, Happy Hollow, Camp Christina and Hilltop Christian Camp. Another is just over the Seelmaer Hill (Gnaw Bone Camp). An organization for black retirees is located here. Another interloper is planning to put foster homes here to house about 75 children full time. Bed and Breakfast operations are springing up all over this area like mushrooms in spring time. Any old timer returning to this area today would not recognize it. Van Buren Township and Brown County in general, is becoming a playground for the rich.

My friend, Olivia Toler, the real estate salesperson who sold us this farm where we now live, and whom I write about in this book, once told me she wished she had a "way back" pill that she could swallow when she came upon old house places when viewing property with clients so she could see how the people lived "way back when." Well, I can tell you, I don't need a pill. I saw much of the way these folks lived when I moved here in 1960. The stories the area residents told me were pretty graphic and I have tried to portray them honestly in this book. I have read the local historical information about this area; I know how the area was formed by the glaciers, etc. Olivia arrived here in 1967 and by that time things were changing fairly quickly.

Van Buren Elementary School's enrollment has nearly tripled and the building has been expanded at least twice, maybe even three times, in my sojourn here. It now educates almost 300 students each year. When our sons started school there, I believe there were only about 130 students enrolled. This shows just how many newcomers have invaded "our" space which they now claim as "their" space.

In the past two years, almost all the changes or improvements—if you can call them that—as seen advertised in legal notices in the local paper concern this area of the county known as Van Buren. It is now, after years of almost total neglect by the county's officials, becoming the fastest changing most desirable part of Brown County in which to live.

Van Buren Elementary School as it looks today.

The former Elkinsville store and post office.

While it was a sad fact of life for most of these earlier people to have to move away, for some it would turn out to be a blessing in disguise. If they had been lucky enough in the past to have gotten factory jobs at RCA or Sarkes-Tarzian in Bloomington; or at Cummins or Arvin's or other factories in Columbus; they could now move to these cities after being ejected by the Corps of Engineers. Moving to the cities where they worked cut down their driving time and gave them more time with their families, putting them closer to emergency services such as hospitals, doctors, law enforcement, shopping, recreation and such.

But still, they missed their old homes and would for years look backward at the society they had enjoyed in these little towns and their environs, attending the township schools, attending church with their relatives and friends and shopping at every little grocery store and with the Peddler Men. Even being reminded of the poverty they lived under does not dampen memories of their childhood.

They have returned on the first Sunday of October now for several years for a reunion with their old neighbors of the Elkinsville and Youno areas.

Everyone is invited to attend this reunion and share a well-filled basket at noon with all attendees. Several former residents have even published a collection of life stories from these residents in book form titled, *"The Town That Was"* and have erected a lovely sign at Elkinsville to mark it the little town that was.

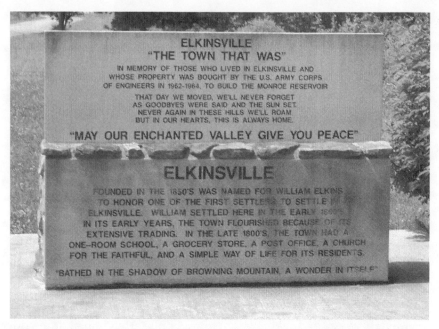

The new Elkinsville sign marks the little town that was, but is no longer.

This is the reverse side of the Elkinsville sign
naming the families that once lived here

Several of the older residents who were removed in this ruthless manner for the reservoir project would not long survive the latest upheaval; many died not long after their removal was an accomplished fact. So many other groups wanted their land, from the governors of Indiana down to people in the cities that needed water to drink and for recreation or wanted a forested place to live, or a place to play, that it would make deep inroads on the private property in Van Buren Township. Most of these old timers could never understand what it was about this place that caused everyone to want to move here, or why they should be moved out of their homes to make way for others.

The residents were kept in a constant uproar and fear of the next person who might want to remove them. Then, too, there had been the Great Depression, WW II, and then the Korean War. For more than a quarter century, from about 1925 until 1955, it was a truly sad time for everyone in Van Buren Township.

The clay soil did not grow much; there wasn't much room to run cattle; very little level farmland; the hillsides were bare for the most part so to some people this land was nearly worthless but to many it was "home." A few years ago in order to avoid paying property tax a few homeowners would quietly slip in extra acreage when selling off some of their land just to get rid of it. This actually was still happening when I moved here. They thought they were being smart and were pulling the wool over the eyes of the buyer; but however little they might have valued their real estate they still did not want to be forced from their land by those in authority for the benefit of others.

We helped Mickey's brother Scott build a ranch house in the bend of 135 in Story in the 1970's. For many years this was the only home within a half-mile radius that had indoor plumbing. It would be a long time before something as simple as indoor bathrooms were common in this area.

When I started my first job as a private secretary in June 1959 at Cummins Engine Company in Columbus I was paid $1.59 per hour; a princely sum for those days. This was just slightly less than my future husband earned after having worked in the factory at Cummins for four years. He would eventually work there six years before he quit and moved on to better paying jobs elsewhere. But from this paltry salary, each of us was fortunate enough to be able to save a small amount from each paycheck. By the time we married we were able to furnish an entire household with new furniture with our savings. This was an incredible accomplishment on our part.

I had been lucky in another area which would help me in this first job of mine. While I had been a senior in high school, the township trustee—who, at that time, was in charge of staffing the schools—had asked me to be the official substitute teacher for grades 1-6 at Clearspring down in Jackson County.

As a reward, since the trustee could not pay me in cash because I was only 16-years-old, still a student, and held no teaching degree, he asked me to buy myself a full wardrobe and bring him the bills. I was able to purchase five dressy outfits plus shoes and coats and these clothes provided me a working wardrobe at Cummins.

The trustee repaid me every penny I had spent and also paid all my senior class expenses for our trip to Washington, D. C. While working at Cummins we were required to dress like a lady every day so these clothes helped me be prepared for the job. I was a good seamstress at that time and was able to purchase nice fabrics and make myself some outfits to extend my wardrobe to meet Cummins' standards.

Money was still tight for us and would remain so until 1965 when I obtained a good-paying job at the Atterbury Job Corps Center near Edinburgh. My extraordinary typing ability and other office skills catapulted me upwards on this job at a tremendous pace and I was soon earning a huge salary for that time. In the first two years I worked at the center my salary more than tripled. We could now live high on the hog!

Mickey had by that time also been able to find a better paying job after leaving Cummins so we survived very well. We were not rich by any means, but after only five or six years of married life we were not doing too badly. We worked very hard and we prospered and others around us were doing the same thing and times really began to improve at last.

These kind, generous and caring people in Van Buren Township welcomed me to this area of Brown County with open arms and loving hearts once they realized I was not uppity as they had suspected I was when I arrived in my finery. They would assist me in many ways over the coming years. Most people meeting me today—even those born and raised in this area—make the incorrect assumption that I am a native Brown Countian. I assure them I am not, and explain that I was adopted at the ripe old age of 18, the age I had attained less than three months before I eloped with Mickey.

Basically, the people of Van Buren Township have always been very self reliant. While people in other areas of the county were calling the sheriff's department with every little complaint about a neighbor or one of his animals, the residents of Van Buren never called in, instead working things out amongst themselves. One glaring incident I can recall occurred in the late 1980's when a tornado went right through the middle of the township, knocking down barns, uprooting trees and doing other damage. No one was hurt or killed during the tornado, but one died the next day while sawing a dangling tree limb down. Not one call went into the sheriff's department about the tornado.

One house was demolished at Stone Head when this huge pine tree was plopped down through the roof into the living area. No one was injured even though four people were inside the home.

During my twenty-one years in the newspaper business in Nashville I interviewed and wrote stories about many people living in Brown County. I enjoyed every minute of those interviews. The joy I saw on the faces of the people I had interviewed when they later read about themselves in the newspaper more than repaid me for my efforts. They loved telling me that people had called or stopped by their homes to tell them what a great story they had told.

Often the pictures I took but did not write a story about were as neat as the life stories of others had been. Sometimes it is the people you should have written about but didn't that you regret the most. That is the primary reason for this book. I should have interviewed these characters prior to their death, now I have to depend upon my memory of them.

At times I observed people doing whatever the chore they had planned for that day happened to be and stopped and took a candid picture without actually writing a story. One of those candid pictures stands out in my mind as one of my best shots.

I was driving between Spearsville and Peoga one Wednesday morning delivering bundles of newspapers to the various stores. It was a warm late spring day when I spied Doreen Hazelgrove—a woman I had never met before—picking fresh pea pods in her garden near Peoga. Slamming on my brakes I picked up the camera I always carried with me, got out and walked into the garden to talk with her

Mrs. Hazelgrove was wearing a flowered dress and she nearly blended in with the wildly flowering pea crop. She wore a granny style apron that she had drawn up from the bottom to form a basket. Into that basket she was placing her freshly picked peas and she agreed that I could take her picture.

I shot the picture, we ran it in the paper, and I sent her a copy of the picture. Later that summer I saw her at the local 4-H fair and asked how she had liked her picture. She replied, "OK, but did you realize I had a bead of sweat on the end of my nose ready to drop off?"

I had not noticed that feature in the picture but when I went back to the office and pulled out my copy of the picture, sure enough, there was that bead of sweat on the end of her nose. To her it may have been embarrassing, but to me it merely showed an attractive woman enjoying the sunshine and bounty of her lovely garden.

Another marvelous lucky shot I took showed what could have been a disaster but turned out to be quite tame. Just after school let out one afternoon a school bus loaded with children was following a loaded log truck up the hill on State Road 135 north of Nashville. The call came over the police monitor I kept near my desk that a school bus had been struck by a log truck. Not knowing what I might find, I grabbed my camera and rushed to the scene.

The air brakes on the loaded log truck had failed part way up the hill about a mile north of town. The quick-thinking school bus driver, seeing that the truck was losing momentum and starting to reverse down the hill, rushed his bus forward against the rear of the log truck and applied his own brakes sharply enough to stop the out-of-control truck.

One log had slipped loose from the center of the load and pushed backward from the load until it just touched the right windshield area of the bus. God was smiling that day and all the children on that bus were safe. After the wheels of the log truck were chocked, the students remained on the bus. I took a picture of the kids hanging out the bus's windows waving at the camera. A disaster averted and a dramatic photo.

My editor at that time, Greg Temple, said every person had a story to tell and urged me to find them so I did. He also said that most people's names would appear in the newspaper only two times in their lives; once when they were born and again when they died.

One year during the 4-H Fair several events were scheduled to involve the children of the county. One of those events was a turtle race. The children could catch a turtle of any type or a terrapin and enter it in a race to win a prize. They would place their turtle in a large circle and the first turtle to scoot outside the large drawn circle won a prize. Once the race was over, the unharmed turtles would be released.

I was there taking pictures of the event when I found this very young boy who was maybe seven or eight years old. He was wearing cut off jeans shorts, no t-shirt and was barefoot if I remember correctly. It was a very hot, sticky July day and he had sweated a lot, mopping his sweaty face and chest with his dirty hands, smearing the dirt everywhere. He had found a tiny quarter-size snapping turtle in the nearby creek and was holding it in his palm to show it to me for a picture. He was going to enter that race and win the prize, he eagerly told me. I took his picture and every dirty smear on that little boy's body showed up in that picture.

I returned to the office and while we were deciding which pictures to run that week I asked that his picture be a part of the fair package and reminded Greg about his telling me about the two times your name appears in print. We used it. That child, when he dies, will have had his name and a picture in the paper three times instead of the customary two.

Over the years I was able to capture many other pictures and stories that gave at least a brief account of the lives of many of Brown County's citizens. One of the women whose husband I had photographed as he was roto-tilling his garden told me one day I was an artist. I had just spent the last few minutes with her in my office telling her how much I liked the oil paintings she created and said I wished I could do that too.

"Oh," she told me, "You are an artist too. You may not use oil paints to create your artworks, but you take wonderful pictures of ordinary people like my husband. You paint your pictures with your words and your camera. You truly are an artist." What an extraordinary compliment she had just given me. If I could remember her name I would tell you who she was. I know where she lived over by Helmsburg but I cannot remember her name.

But it was sometimes the interview that I never got around to doing; the story I never wrote and the picture I didn't take, that nowadays means the most to me.

It reminds me of Pete Schrougham, a Korean veteran who lives on Salt Creek Road. I once interviewed Pete for a veteran's memorial special section and he became one of my favorite interviews because even though he spent his time in Korea, he received a head wound and had not a single memory of the time he spent there.

My friend Pete Schrougham.

The interview he gave me consisted of his showing me pictures of his war buddies and other activities; at least he assumed they were his buddies. He was in pictures with men he didn't remember in uniforms in a war and he had no recollection of their names. Local friends had told him how he arrived home from the war and in what manner he arrived and he related those tales to me. A strange interview for sure, but a fascinating one.

Pete is still with us and keeps busy these days doing volunteer work for the sheriff department's TRIAD program which checks on the welfare of the elderly. He also donates lots of time to the veteran's affairs office doing whatever needs doing for the county's veterans like placing flags on the graves of veterans and other chores.

Into this collection of stories about people I have met during my sojourn in Brown County I can add dozens more names. All of them had stories to tell, but I just knew them so well I guess I assumed everyone else did also, so I never asked them for an interview. But now as I look back I believe that is not the case, not everyone knew these people as intimately as I did. I should have written about them long ago while they were alive to tell their own stories. Now I have to rely on my memories and the memories of those they left behind and I'm not sure our memories are any better than Pete Schrougham's.

One of our friends is Virgil Keith Floyd of Nashville. He is a true eccentric in the best way. He loves to restore old vehicles and drives one wherever he goes. His vehicles are the ones these old timers in this book would remember and love. If you are lucky enough to be admitted to his home, please take notice of the restored Model A (maybe it is a Model T) convertible that sits in his living room. From its front seat he can watch his television set in comfort and he has built a table for holding books, food and drinks across the top of the passenger's door. We recently saw him driving on State Road 46 headed toward Columbus. We flagged him down and I took the following picture.

Don't you just love Virgil Floyd's old car.

Many of these people in Van Buren had an impact on my life in one way or another. Some helped me raise our sons by feeding them or watching out for them when I was not around. I never knew that until those same two sons started telling me about them after they were grown men. Others did other kind things for me or my family that was never acknowledged with a story or photograph. Some just made me laugh and some told the most marvelous tales and stories I ever heard.

When one sits down to revisit their memories of an earlier Brown County you can see how the interaction of one family weaves into the memories of another family. As you tell one's story, you can see where it leads to a tie-in to another one's story through marriage and/or friendship to another family. It shows how perhaps a mile or two was far enough for these early modern people to go to meet someone they could love a lifetime.

Look for parallels in the Fleetwood-Carmichael families; Ayers-Wilkerson families; Fleetwood-Ayers families; the Fleetwood-Hedrick families; Carmichael-Lucas families, and others. While each is a separate story of a separate family, they are so intertwined the stories could have been condensed into one. For clarity I have tried to separate the groupings.

In this book I would like to give the fame of acknowledgment to those Van Buren Township people in hopes that their stories and their deeds will be remembered by others who loved these people as much as I did. We will start with stories about the residents of the Story community since that is where I lived with my little family in four locations for about 20 years.

My husband was born in a log cabin where the gray ranch house is now located inside the curve of State Road 135 as it bends to the south in Story. That old house burned down when he was a young boy. The Story sagas and others truly are, I believe, the stuff of legends.

Aquilla Moore

One of the first persons I met when I married my husband, Mickey Ayers, and moved to Brown County in 1960 was Aquilla Moore. Mickey and I were living in Story at the time I met Aquilla who actually lived just outside Pikes Peak on Poplar Grove Road. But since we lived at Story at the time, I am starting with Aquilla Moore.

Quiller, as everyone called him, was a farmer and a dedicated Democrat party worker who took his job very seriously. I had just turned 18-years-old when I married but Quiller did not know that. Mickey and I had scarcely settled in when he knocked on our door one day, introduced himself and told me he was the precinct committeeman for our township. At that time one could not vote at the age of 18 so I had to tell him that he would not be able to register me to vote.

Amazingly enough he kept track of my age for the next three years and just after my 21st birthday he returned to our home and registered me to vote. He was not going to give the Republican Party a chance to register me. I guess that is one of the reasons the Democratic Party has made such a strong showing of winning candidates over the decades; they had dedicated committeemen like Quiller.

"Quiller" Moore stands beside the stone grinding wheel that Henry Cross once owned and used. His faithful dog, Bullet, keeps him company.

Quiller's daughter, Maxine Bailey, lives in Bellsville and continues to work for the party, serving as the county Democratic Party treasurer. His other daughter, Phyllis, is married to Marvin Stone and they live just south of the now deceased Quiller's property on Poplar Grove Road.

Maxine Bailey of Bellsville with her daughters, Theresa, (L) and Joyce.

Marvin and Phyllis Stone live at the juncture of
Hamilton Creek and Poplar Grove Roads.

Quiller not only registered me to vote he called me many times with story and picture ideas for the newspaper, many of which turned into good copy for the newspaper. He was convinced I could do just about anything he asked me to do.

He called me at work one day and asked if I would be stopping by Crouch's Market in Pike's Peak on the way home from work. By this time we lived in Becks Grove and I had to drive past Crouch's every evening on the way home. I had not planned to stop but told him I could if he needed me to stop by. He wanted to talk to me about something very serious he said.

Quiller's wife, Laverne Moore.

When I got to Pikes Peak that afternoon he pulled me aside and said he wanted me to apply for the job of county highway superintendent which was open at that time. "You have more sense than anybody in this county. I want you to apply for the job," he said. I was so startled at his suggestion I was nearly speechless (for one time in my life).

Although over the years I had written many editorials concerning our road systems and offering many free personal—and, I thought, very helpful even if biased—opinions of how the roads could be better maintained, I had never considered actually taking on the job. I told Quiller he needed to find a man with more experience than I had to do this work. I forget now who eventually got the job, it might have been Jim Kelp, but things began to improve as far as the county highway system was concerned.

It is dedicated people like Quiller which makes the folks in Van Buren Township real standouts in my opinion.

Quiller and Laverne are buried in the Mellott Cemetery on Poplar Grove Road.

Story's Clotha

As a journalist I was trained to recognize that every person you met had at least one story (their own) to tell and I found many of those stories during the 21 years I worked as a newspaper writer. I wrote so many stories about ordinary citizens of our fair county that it would be impossible to remember them all. At this late date, I just wish I had kept copies of all those "ordinary" individuals' stories that, as it turned out, were not so ordinary after all.

One of the stories I never got around to writing concerned the life of a woman who was born, reared and lived in the Story community of Brown County, Indiana, her entire life. Her name was Clotha (pronounced locally as Clothie) Hedrick Robertson and she certainly added to the color and vitality of our small community. I don't know why I never wrote about Clothie because she was a wonderful friend over the years. I believe another of the Democrat's staff writers, the late Dick Reed, wrote about Clothie, but he did not know her as intimately as I did so my memories of her will be a little different than Dick's.

Clotha Hedrick.

In my opinion, Clothie was born two or three generations later than she should have been born. Her total character fit another era much better than the one in which she actually lived. She was a fairly stout woman and always wore dresses which struck her about mid calf. Every dress I can remember her wearing had gold or brown in the floral patterns and all were made using the same pattern seems like. She always wore sturdy lace up "granny-style" shoes with tan cotton stockings year 'round.

Clothie also wore the same kind of stockings on her arms when she was outside working in her yard or garden. First she would cut herself a thumb hole in the end of the old sock, then snip off enough little pinches of the rest of the sock's toes that the stocking would fit her like a glove. She would pull the long stocking up over her entire arm to prevent any sunlight from hitting her skin. Only her fingers would remain exposed to the sun.

On her head she wore a cotton bonnet, usually a floral patterned one, which had a large bib that stuck out several inches in front to shield her face. She never wore makeup and had beautiful skin tones and textures.

The only reason I can think of as to why she dressed like this was perhaps she had read about skin cancer and wanted to protect herself. I would hate to think she did this just to raise our curiosity level. She had a wicked laugh and I can just image her laughing if she thought we were curious about her.

Susan (Suz) Hedrick

For decades the Hedrick family owned and operated the Story General Store. The family depended upon Clothie, the spinster sister who lived just across the road from the store tending her elderly mother, Susan "Suz," to operate it. Sometimes Suz would sit in the store with Clothie to keep her company and visit with those who stopped by to purchase something.

Suz and Clothie were sitting talking together inside the store one day when I, as a new mom with baby Lonnie in my arms, proudly showed the squirming bundle to them. I told them the baby's name and opened the blanket so they could see him. Suz took one look at that baby and said "Little Mick," and that was how she referred to him as long as she lived. Since Suz had known Mickey since he was Lonnie's size I never corrected her but I could never see that resemblance she and so many others saw.

At other times, Clothie could sit in the comfort of her living room with her mother and wait until she saw a car drive up to the store, or a pedestrian step upon the porch, then she would ease herself out of her chair and start slowly plodding very deliberately toward the store at a leisurely walk. We learned to stand on the porch and wait for her to get there and open the store. Clothie never hurried and she never ran and she always gave you a smile when she got there. Her smile was worth the wait.

Crown on Story Store gas pump.

Perhaps we needed to buy some gasoline from her tall red gas pumps with their white crowns. Those two pumps sat just off the porch at the front of the store. Or, maybe we needed some kerosene with which to start a fire. She had that on the porch also. The kerosene tank was below the floor somewhere, maybe in the basement. There was a crank for lifting the kerosene into the top part of the apparatus on the porch and she would turn the black oil-encrusted crank until a gallon or so was raised into the upper tank, then let it down into our containers. This manual pump had been there for years but was still accurate to the penny.

Inside the store one could see remnants of history past and current, but certainly not of the future. Clothie had shoes in boxes that had been there so long the boxes had turned color and the leather of the shoes had cracked and were no longer in style. One of the men I had interviewed while I worked at the newspaper told a funny story.

Johnny Brand was a wee little fellow who lived in Brand Hollow near the tiny village of Pikes Peak which was about seven miles east of Story. When he got his induction orders for World War II he appeared at the Selective Service System ready and raring to go. They took one look, weighed him in at 86 pounds and sent him back home, telling him to "go home and grow some," he laughingly told me.

Laughing as he told me this story with his bright blue eyes alight with merriment, he exclaimed, "I came home but I never grew any more."

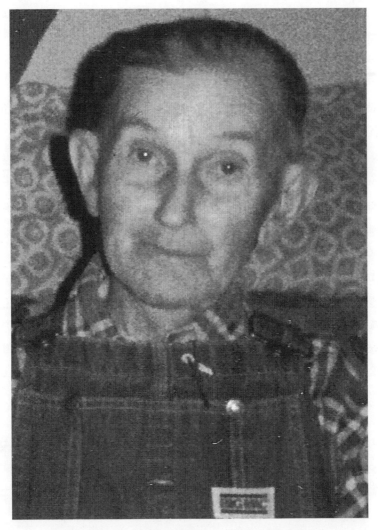

Johnny Brand tried to break in a pair of shoes for
fifty years that he bought from Clothie.

Johnny had worked for the highway department before his retirement cutting weeds and grass along the roadway which ran through Story. He had bought a pair of shoes and had been breaking them in for a long time, he told me. He didn't state it, but I am willing to bet he had bought that pair of brogans from Clothie Hedrick.

"How long have you had them," I asked when he returned to the porch with the offending shoes in hand.

"Fifty years," he laughed. He had kept them polished and in pride of place in his living room all those years attempting to break in that leather.

Inside the Story Store, on shelves of a cabinet extending out into the rear of the store, were tins of ointments in little bins, medicines for cows' udders and other pesky problems around the farm. Like those shoes the store had for sale, these tins too had undoubtedly been there for generations.

If it was a blustery day, we might walk across the loudly creaking wood floor to the back of the store and stand with our behinds turned towards the roaring fire Clotha kept in a huge pot bellied stove back there during the winter. She hated to be cold and always came across the road dressed like an Eskimo when someone needed in the store on wintry days so that fire stayed pretty warm. That was no small trick either. The inside of the store was large and open, with tin on both the inside and the outside, and with none of the insulation we have and take for granted today in its walls, floors or ceiling.

Clothie would walk with us back to the stove area then go behind the long wooden counter and ask what we needed. She always kept chocolate haystack candy during the holiday season so we might order 50 cents worth of that. She would add a counterweight to her little scale, pick up a little copper scoop and start dropping in what she though would be 50 cents worth into the badly scratched copper hopper. It would have taken many years of candy sliding against that copper hopper to scratch it up like it was. Usually she was right on the money. It would be interesting to know just how many pounds of haystack candy she sold over the many years she operated the store.

But maybe we were hungry for something other than candy on this visit. We might order two slices of minced ham and a slice of longhorn cheese. Clothie would pick up a butcher's knife with a heavy blade at least a foot long and start slicing. She could slice through that big round of meat and cheese with the skill of a butcher, making the slices exactly the same thickness. We paid by the slice, not the pound also. I probably would have cut my arm off with that knife had I tried to use it as she did.

Or, perhaps we might ask for a chunk of her "pickled dog". "How big a piece do you want," she would demand and we would point through the jar at the size piece we wanted. She had cut the meat to a size to fit any appetite.

Now this really wasn't dog meat, it was just that Clothie called it pickled dog. It was actually small round link bologna which she had bought in bulk, chopped into various sized pieces and pickled with her secret recipe. With each order she forked out of the jar, she would hand you four saltine squares. If you thought you wanted more crackers you had to ask for them. She might look at you askance, but she would give you a couple more. In her opinion you should only need four saltines. The saltines were doled out with the minced ham and cheese also.

No one bothered to ask if her hands were clean when she handled candy, crackers or minced ham and cheese. We just assumed they were, accepted our offerings like manna from heaven after we had paid for them, and started munching. She never used sterile food handling gloves as they have to do now and she never poisoned any of us that I know of.

*A much younger Clothie Hedrick stands in front of what
we believe to be either the Story School or church.*

City folks who were lost on our county's back roads occasionally found themselves in her store quite by accident. Usually they were looking for pop or drinking water or asking directions on how to get back to where they needed to be. If they just wanted a drink of cold water, she would point them outside to the tall hand pump beside the store. It came equipped with an aluminum can which had held Vienna sausages in a previous life, but was used now to catch and hold drinking water when you pumped the handle. It was attached with a fairly long, thin and flexible wire that went through a small hole punched through the top lip of the can and attached at the other end to the pump so it would not be lost. Everyone drank from the same cup because there was nowhere to buy bottled Evian water. You just rinsed the dust out of the cup, pumped fresh water in and drank.

If her customers were lost she would give them directions with a smile (accurate ones too) then ask if they would like to try some of her pickled dog. She always had to explain what it was before they would try it. After all, this was a back woods county and Story was even further back in the woods than most little towns. And Clothie, bless her soul, was about as back woodsy as you could get, but there wasn't a better person that I ever met than she. I'm sure some of these city folks would not have been surprised to learn that the meat in this back woods store really was dog meat, but I assure you it was not.

Many of these city folks fell in love with Clothie's pickled dog after they dared to taste it. Some would later write her (she had no phone) and ask that she pickle and ship a gallon or so to them. Clothie did a pretty brisk business in this manner. She would be dead and gone before we realized just how far her fame had traveled.

Clothie was courted by her beau, Sherman Robertson, for 48 years before they married. They were ever faithful and saw each other several times a week for brief chats and went for a ride in his car once a week, usually on Sunday. Everyone who knew them teased them about their courtship but both would deny until the day they married that they were anything more than just acquaintances.

If questioned about this, Clothie would chuckle and her beau would just grunt and refuse to answer.

Both Clothie and her intended were left by their siblings to care for each of their elderly mothers. Clothie's mother, Susan (Suz) Hedrick, lived to be 95 years old. She was born in 1869 and died in 1964, 24 years after her husband Albert "Pink" Hedrick had died.

Albert (Pink) and Suz Hedrick.

After Suz died Sherman did not want Clothie to live alone so they finally married. Sherman lived about a tenth of a mile away to the East so he moved her in with him and his mother, Flora whom everyone called Toy, also lived to be about 93 or 94 years old. I had wanted to shivaree them but was afraid someone might be shot because Sherman was not known for his good humor, so we never dared to do that for them.

Sherman's mother, Toy, was one of Grandma Lizzie's many sisters. Most of her life had been spent inside first one doctor's office or another. Apparently she was somewhat of a hypochondriac. But, then again, maybe she wasn't. Maybe all those doctor's visits were what allowed her to enjoy such a long life span. Mickey used to have a lot of fun with his great Aunt Toy.

Toy Robertson in her mop cap. She was a sister of Grandma Lizzie and my husband's great aunt.

Once a very young Mickey and Toy decided they would make themselves some wings and go for a flyover. They worked diligently for many hours over several days constructing a set of wings for each of them. First they laid some small sticks out to the shape they wanted their wings to be. Then they carefully glued on lots of newspapers and a few chicken feathers just for good measure.

One windy day they thought they were ready to take to the air. There was a long, cleared hillside next to Toy and Sherman's house. Toy and Mickey chose this as their launch site and trudged up the hillside carrying their wings. Once they got to the top they helped each other strap on the wings and when all was ready they started flapping their wings like mad as they ran down this hillside. I can just see them now. A little boy and this very old but still spry woman running down the hill, probably yelling like crazy, "See me fly."

The day was so windy that after only a short run down the hill, the wind tore their wings all to pieces. Dejected but laughing hard, the two returned home to ponder their next flight of fancy.

One time our sons had gone for a walk across a fallow corn field with their dog on a leash. When they returned from their walk the dog was running free and an adult groundhog was on the leash, tame as it could be. Our dog started bothering the groundhog when we turned it loose so it could leave. We tried to stop it but the large dog we had at that time finally killed the groundhog.

Mickey took the groundhog out into a field near us, dug a hole and buried the thing so the dogs could not dig it up.

Shortly after the proper funeral and burial of the groundhog Sherman paid a call on us and we sat out in our newly finished garage talking with him. Our dog licked him on his hands as we told him the story about the groundhog and no one thought any more about it.

A short time after he went home Sherman called us and asked that we dig up the groundhog and have it checked for rabies since our dog had licked his hand. What an inconvenience to us that was but we complied. We had to drive that groundhog's head all the way to the Indiana Health Department in Indianapolis where it was tested and found to be healthy. That story was told just to show what a sourpuss Sherman could be at times. He was always kind of a curmudgeon and that is the main reason we did not shivaree them when they married.

Another cute story about Sherman occurred when he called me to say he had some fresh eggs I could have if one of the boys would stop by and pick them up. I sent Lonnie to his house to get them but he returned empty handed. "There was something wrong with them," was all he said.

Sherman called, actually laughing for once, and explained that his hens were the varieties that laid eggs of several different colors. Some of his hens laid light blue, green, brown, speckled or white eggs, he said. Lonnie refused to have anything to do with those eggs. This incident proves that Sherman could laugh if something struck his funny bone, but most of the time he was quiet and surly.

Clothie was a good cook and loved to bake apple and cherry turnovers. One summer after she married Sherman I was taking my sons for a walk when she came out on her porch and called us into her house.

This scene could have been taken from Clothie Robertson's kitchen. George Bredewater merely used his imagination.

"I have been making apple turnovers today and made way too many for us. I guess I got carried away. You and the boys come in and eat some of them," she laughed and invited us inside.

They were mouth-wateringly delicious and we ate our share. They were warm from the oven, stuffed with either cinnamon flavored apples or sweet cherries and had white icing drizzled all over them. The boys offered to do some chores for her in exchange for her hospitality, but she demurred. It seemed she only wanted our company for however short or long a time we could stay. How nice that was. She invited us to sit on the porch with her and visit for awhile more so we did. After that, any time we were walking by and she was baking turnovers, she would invite us in to share them. How could we refuse her? Someone had to help her eat those tarts, why not us. She certainly never had to ask us twice I can tell you.

The Robertsons shared several years of married life together before and after his own mother died until he contracted lung cancer.

Sherman died July 31, 1984 a few weeks after surgery. Clothie lived on in a mobile home her family placed next to her nephew's house about a mile away to the East for several years after Sherman was gone. Like her mother Suz, Clothie was in her 90s when she passed away, thus ending a saga of friendship that began many years earlier. Clotha and all the Hedricks are buried in the McKinney Cemetery just off State Road 135 south.

After Sherman died and she was living in her mobile home I asked Clothie if she would share her recipe for pickled dog with me. It took some persuasion on my part and some hard thinking on hers before she would share it, but finally she did. My husband now makes a small batch about once a month for us to enjoy. I hope you enjoy eating some of Clothie's Pickled Dog and learning a little about the interesting person who developed this taste treat. Don't forget your saltine crackers.

Story General Store's Pickled Dog

The following recipe was given to me many years ago by Clotha Hedrick who operated the Story General Store in Brown County, Indiana. Clothie sold hundreds of gallons of her personally prepared pickled dog (really ring bologna) over the years. She had a fairly steady clientele from Chicago and Cincinnati that she shipped the delicious meat to. These folks had at one time or another stopped by her store, tasted the goodie, and asked that she prepare and ship it to them.

Each time you walked into her store and asked for pickled dog, which she kept out on her long wooden counter, she would grab a long-handled fork, open the jar and spear you a piece, placing it in a small brown grocery sack. She would also hand you four saltine crackers to go with your snack.

Clothie's cardinal rule for making pickled dog was "never touch the meat" with your own hands because doing so would cause the vinegar to "die." To prepare pickled dog she speared a ring of bologna with a long fork, placed the meat on a cutting board, then cut it into chunks with her long butcher knife and placed the pieces in her big jar with the long fork. So DON'T TOUCH THE MEAT WITH YOUR HANDS if you try to make it yourself or blame me if you do touch it and your vinegar "dies".

Here's how she made it. We make it all the time and it is delicious.

Find a good brand of <u>ring</u> bologna and chop it into small chunks and place the pieces into a big jar. When the jar is full, add two tablespoons of mixed pickling spices and one whole dried red pepper <u>per gallon of meat.</u> A teaspoon of dried red pepper flakes also works we have found. Add enough cold distilled vinegar to completely cover the meat. Set aside for 2 or 3 days, then enjoy. That's it.

She always used the most inexpensive brand of plain distilled vinegar she could buy, but that is no longer available in our area. All we can find is the apple flavored or white vinegar variety, but it all works about as well. The apple cider flavored one will leave a slight apple flavor to the meat. Clothie always used the Eckrich brand of ring bologna. You can buy it by the piece at most large grocery stores but it is kind of expensive this way. She would order it by the 10- or 20-pound box and the Eckrich delivery truck would bring it to her that way. Never stint on the meat's quality and don't use beef bologna because that is one of the secrets of good pickled dog. The jars of meat that are prepared and sold commercially cannot compare with that made by your own hand. The commercial brand is kind of pink looking and the meat is squishier than this old fashioned pickled dog. Stick with the good stuff.

Lizzie Wilkerson

Grandma Lizzie was my husband Mickey's maternal grandmother, Lizzie Ayers Wilkerson. She lived in Story as long as I knew her. She was one of those unique people whose quirks and foibles should have been recorded for posterity but so far have not been.

She was an Ayers girl who married a Wilkerson man (Grover). Grover died in 1958 before I met my future husband. He had had a car wreck coming home from work, and died a couple of weeks later of a stroke. Their daughter, Lenore (my mother-in-law) was a Wilkerson girl who married an Ayers man (Donald).

This was a common occurrence in this area of the world prior to most people having dependable transportation. When you wanted to wed, you just walked over the hillside to the next home to find a mate. Sometimes those mates might be your distant cousins but if they were not close cousins being related wasn't so bad.

There were all kinds of cousins to choose from. There were double cousins (those children that ensued when two brothers of one family married two sisters in another); first cousins, second cousins, third cousins, long-lost cousins and kissing cousins. Then there was the person who was a first cousin to your first cousin, but was no relation to you. That was a safe one to marry.

This was equally true in other parts of Brown County and elsewhere at that time in our history. Once you wed them you might start thinking, "Gee, did I get mixed up and wed my brother, if so did I somehow become my own grandma?"

This is a copy of the receipt for membership in the Improved Order of Red Man's Lodge in Bellsville paid in 1920. This $1.25 paid Grover's dues through June 1924.

Lizzie was born into a really large family of children, but she would have only three children of her own, Clifford, Amos and Lenore. Amos, 83, is the only survivor at this writing and lives with his wife of 61 years, Olive Moore Wilkerson, near Spurgeon's Corner.

*The Redman's Lodge in Bellsville. It burned in the
later years of the last century but for scores of years
was the meeting place for many lodge members.*

Some of Lizzie's sisters would have nearly a dozen children so there were many relatives when I married into this early Brown County family. A couple of her sisters married Greathouse men who also came from really large families so we were related to many, many people. Sadly, most of them are now dead and gone.

My husband and some of his friends, his brother Scott and our own children would spend lots of time with Lizzie. Since she babysat our boys at times she actually reared, or helped to rear, several more than her own three children.

Grandma Lizzie Wilkerson, holds a grandson, Dewayne.

I don't have a really good picture of Grandma Lizzie, but if you can picture in your mind's eye Granny Clampitt of the 1960's Beverly Hillbillies television show, you could be looking at a clone of Grandma Lizzie. The two women were identical in appearance and manner of dress. Actress Irene Dunne's character could have been designed from a picture of Grandma herself they looked and acted so much the same. And in a way, even their voices were very similar.

Grandma Lizzie was totally self-sufficient to her dying day. She had once ridden on a motorcycle and loved it. This was fine until she saw a couple wreck a motorcycle while riding one right along beside her as she walked there in Story. They were skinned up pretty badly and their leather clothing was torn nearly to shreds. That ended her wanting to ride a cycle. This was a woman who would only ride with me to town in a car if she absolutely could not find another person to drive her.

She liked to go to a larger town such as Seymour or Columbus to shop at least once a month and since she did not drive, someone had to drive for her. She had her own car (a '57 Chevrolet) but never learned to drive, always depending upon others to do that for her. I was always her last choice for driver. Since I was an accident-free driver I never understood her attitude.

When she was my passenger, she would sit on her side of the car with one hand on the arm rest gripping it so tightly her knuckles were white and the other hand on the door handle. I almost expected her to bail out at any moment. If I went over 40 MPH she would accuse me of speeding and tell me to slow down. Since these times were pre-seatbelt days, I would slow down to keep her safely seated in the car.

When we married, Mickey and I lived in the house just south of Clothie's house in Story. Grandma visited us most days for at least a few minutes and drove me to distraction. You see, when we married I could not cook. I could bake cornbread but nothing else. I guess she worried about Mickey starving because nearly every day she would bring a small bowl of food for him and say, "Here is something for Mick's supper," as she handed it to me. There was only enough for one person in that bowl and that used to make me so mad I could have spit. But her trickery paid off, I had to learn to cook and over the next 15 years or so I tried to perfect at least a dish or two that I could be proud of. Now, 46 years later, I'm still learning but at least the food I cook is edible and we never starve.

She once told me the story of what she had bought Mickey for his ninth birthday present. Keep in mind that he was born at the tail end of the great depression in October 1937 and so would have turned nine about 1946. Times were still very difficult for the Ayers family and most others in this neighborhood.

Mick's father Donald served on Okinawa and his family of wife and four kids living alone became nearly destitute before he returned. Mickey had always loved pork and beans; going so far as to make pork and bean sandwiches when he could get some, so that gave Grandma an idea for his ninth birthday present. She told me she bought him a large can of pork and beans and would not make him share them with anyone else. Knowing how he still loves them and Vienna sausage today, I'm pretty sure that by day's end they were all gone. Now that is a birthday present never to be forgotten.

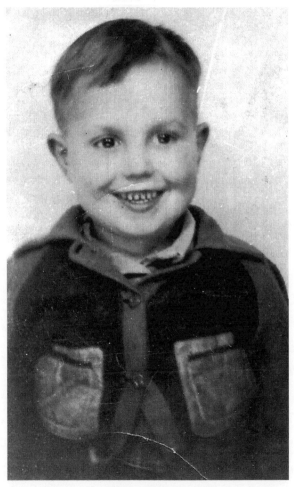

A very young Mickey appears to be very happy with his new coat.

For another birthday when he was very young, maybe three or four years old, she gave him a new coat. He looks to be about three years old and very pleased with himself when his picture was taken while wearing it. I am including that picture here.

Grandma was a busy woman on a daily basis. There was not another member of the neighborhood, male or female, who worked more or harder every day than she did. One might see her walking— her favorite means of transportation—across a farmer's field in early spring with a bucket on one arm as she scouted for wild greens. On other days she might be working in her garden. I have seen her pushing a one-row cultivator for hours on end; a job that would be hard for a man, but she did it regularly. This cultivator had a large front wheel, with a framework that held handles, and a single shovel to turn the earth. They are difficult even for a man to push but I have seen Lizzie push one of them for hours and hours.

She loved eating fresh vegetables and grew almost everything she needed. She had a tiny strawberry patch that I loved to raid before my brother-in-law Scott discovered they were ripe. Grandma would yell at me to "git out of them strawberries" and I would reluctantly leave them. They were luscious to eat fresh but she wanted them for pies and jams.

Lizzie had her regular garden behind her house where she grew beans, corn and potatoes and other things such as cabbage for her table vegetables. Another large garden for potatoes and lots of sweet corn was located where Scott built his house. When this garden behind her house was plowed and prepared for planting with a tractor, it left about a five foot strip around the field. It was in those strips that the strawberries, green onions, leaf lettuce and other delicacies could be found that she had planted.

Other days might find her out on the porch doing her laundry in the Maytag washer Grover purchased for her on Valentine's Day 1947 for $19.95. The washer was bought from the Simmens Hardware Store in Columbus. When going through family pictures I found a copy of the receipt where Grover had purchased the machine which I used occasionally when I first wed. Originally the Maytag was powered by a gas engine but it was later converted to an electric motor so she could do her laundry inside the covered porch.

Receipt for a new Maytag washer that Grover Wilkerson bought for Grandma Lizzie on Valentine's Day, 1947.

She would also go into the woods and pick wild grapes to make jelly and jams or find an apple tree and pick up the droppings. When she made her jelly, she never used fruit pectin but instead would boil the juices down until it jelled on its own, making it extremely full flavored.

Grandma never bought syrup, instead making her own by boiling down sugar and water then adding maple flavoring when it was thick enough to pour on her pancakes. This only took a few minutes so the syrup was always fresh.

Grandma Lizzie is flanked by her daughter Lenore
Ayers and Lenore's son, Richard.

On the left side of the big garden area in that narrow edging left by the tractor were her chicken pens. She liked to raise her own poultry and have the fresh eggs so she could always be counted on to have a dozen or so hens in residence along with a rooster or two. Each spring she would let one or two hens "set" or brood a clutch of eggs so she never had to buy fresh chicks to renew her flock. The brooding hens supplied her with fresh batches of chicks every year. She always had fresh chicken meat when she wanted it and fresh eggs as needed.

If you have ever raised chickens you know that at least one of two of them will be rejected by the rest of the flock. The other chickens will peck at and pull the feathers from the outcast until, if they are not stopped, the outcast is actually plucked to death. To prevent this

Grandma Lizzie would isolate the picked-on hen then cut herself a limber switch and keep it handy. It was not unusual to wake up in her extra bedroom in the morning and hear her yelling at her bad, bad hens as she switched them for picking on the outcast. I nearly fell out of the bed laughing the first time I saw her whipping her chickens with a switch and talking to them like they were naughty children.

This nice plump rooster, drawn by George Bredewater, appears to be just about the right size to be made into chicken and dumplings.

Recently a local realtor, Karen Zody, (by the way she is also a first cousin, Aunt Susie's daughter) was at our house and she mentioned that a property she had listed had a Lizzie-built building on it. Puzzled we asked Karen what she meant and she explained that as long as she could remember if Grandma Lizzie needed a building or pen built she would grab up any piece of lumber or board she could find and start nailing it together.

She never measured or cut a board to size; she just nailed it together, made it fit and then found some roofing material to place over it. We then understood what Karen meant because this description fit Grandma to a T. Her finished buildings might not be architecturally attractive but they were certainly eye-catching, interesting and served their intended purpose.

Grandma didn't have to buy much feed for her "free range" chickens. She had an electric range she rarely used sitting on her enclosed back porch, because most of the time she preferred to use her black wood-fired cookstove which sat in the kitchen. On that stove she kept a couple of three-quart black iron pots with handles. As she prepared her own daily food all vegetable scraps such as apple or potato peelings, left over bread or cakes and pies, and pounded egg shells etc. would be added to one pot of water and cooked until the scraps were soft and mushy. This would be her chicken feed for the next day after it had cooled.

She rarely had anything to throw away or discard seemed like. She had a use for every leftover. She would roll over laughing today if she could see the price of eggs in the up-scale grocery stores that sell the much touted "free-range" chicken eggs because they "are better." She actually was a futurist and didn't know it.

In the other pot was the daily ration of soup beans. These pots of beans graced the wood cookstove of nearly every resident of the area. Any time of day or night, soup beans would be ready to eat.

And, if you looked in the pie safe, you were most likely to find what was left of a pone of cornbread to go with your beans and a slice or two of homemade pie.

Going into her kitchen was like visiting a little house on the prairie that was full of antiques. Grandma was not an antiques collector; it was just that everything she owned was old and well worn.

A large round oak dining table sat kind of off center to one side. It had claw feet and a single round pedestal in the center to hold it up. It was always covered with some kind of pretty oilcloth cover so it could be wiped clean easily after each meal. Right in the center stood the salt and pepper shakers which were shaped like little ears of corn and were green on the bottom and parts of the sides, and bright yellow ridges on the rest of it. In reality, the shakers did look just like miniature ears of corn. There was always a pretty vase of some kind sitting there which held the table cutlery. All this was covered by a very pretty, hand-embroidered tablecloth when not in use to keep the flies off.

An old toaster sat there too but it was like no toaster you will find today. You could toast two slices at once by turning a little wooden knob on one end which would open each side to allow you to lay a slice of bread inside. You would then close it up and turn it on (it was an electric one). Occasionally you would open the side to see if the toast was done.

A tin door pie safe that had perhaps four shelves inside it stood against one wall behind the table. Above that there was a single wooden cabinet which was painted turquoise. These safes and cabinets held all the plates, cups and saucers and left-over foods for another meal. The wood fired cookstove stood to the right of the table up against the living room wall and then there was a small stand which held a wash pan and dishrags for cleanup. A bucket of fresh water was always sitting there beside the wash pan and a towel hung nearby on a nail to dry your hands on. In winter it was common in the mornings to find the bucket contained a solid chunk of ice since the fires did not last through the night.

A chopping block was a common sight among the homes of yesteryear.

The refrigerator stood on the enclosed porch with the electric range. It was rounded at the top and stood up on four legs and was called an icebox or Frididaire even though it was not made to hold ice, but was electric. No matter the actual brand might have been, GE, Amana or another, they were referred to as a Frigidaire.

She did not have an indoor bathroom or running water. A hand pump sat just outside her kitchen door for water and that was handy enough for her. Water was carried inside in a galvanized bucket several times each day. She thought it was "nasty" for people to go to the toilet inside their homes and always used her outdoor john with the half moon cut in the door and the Sears Roebuck catalog on the seat beside her.

George Bredewater drew this picture of an old hand pump.
Grandma had one just like it just outside the kitchen door.

The toilet sat at the far right end of her garden on a piece of that five-foot strip of land surrounding her main garden. It was camouflaged with blooming hollyhocks which the bees buzzed regularly. There might be a snake or other infestation in the john but she didn't care or worry about such things, because everything had to beware of her. It could be a real wake up call first thing in the morning to visit the necessary house at Grandma's.

A new friend of ours that we just met a week ago gave me
this snapshot of her outdoor toilet. This one is a little fancier
made than Grandma Lizzie's and had no hollyhocks.

Grandma's own house was made from very small logs, stuffed with homemade chinking consisting of anything she could find to mix together that would stick in the spaces between the logs. This might include shredded newspaper or cardboard softened in water with flour and starch added as a binding agent or mud mixed with straw. Both the ceilings and the walls were then wallpapered with whatever could be found at the Murphy's Five and Ten Cent Store in Seymour. Whatever wallpaper roll remnants could be found and purchased cheaply, whether they matched each other or not, would be used and the homemade water, flour and starch mixture was used to paste it to the walls.

It is a wonder her place didn't burn down years before it actually did but it stood as long as she needed it. Her house burned while another relative lived in it after her death. Every wall in that house had at least a dozen layers of wallpaper on it. She kept a pot bellied stove in her living room for heating her house. It was her habit to lay in some paper, a few sticks of kindling and a bunch of kerosene. Sometimes when she built a fire there would already be some hot coals in the bottom and this would cause the kerosene fumes to start smoking. When she threw that lighted match to this, instant combustion happened and with a big loud "whoomp" the fire belched outward through the open door, the stove jumped upwards a few inches and the fire was started. The stove's sides would soon glow cherry red.

The same house lot now has a house we built for another relative, our Aunt Ann (really Anna Elizabeth Ayers Pruitt) and her husband Jim Pruitt and their brown Chihuahua "Iffin." Ann was the only sister to my husband's father, Don Ayers, and was the daughter of Arnold and Myrtie Ayers.

The Pruitts are long dead and lie in the Mt. Zion Cemetery. Iffin got his name from the fact that iffin you didn't give him room and stay out of his space he would bite a chunk out of your leg. My boys were terrified of this little dog.

He would bark madly at everyone who came to their house and Ann would scold him and send him to the bedroom. That smart mouthed little dog would go to the bedroom as he was told, but would look back over his shoulder several times as he left the room and give both us and his mistress another growl or bark and keep right on going, his toenails making clicking sounds on the linoleum floor with each step he took.

Anna Elizabeth (Ann) Ayers Pruitt.

The house we helped build for the Pruitts is now part of the Story Store's Bed and Breakfast enterprise as are all the houses there now except for the one we helped Scott build.

When Grandma babysat our boys while we went fishing or were otherwise occupied, she would hold them in her lap as she sat in her rocking chair and sing dirty ditties to them for lullabies at the top of her lungs. I swear she could remember every ditty or poem she had ever learned. As was the custom back when she attended school, memorization was the way they learned and she never forgot a single line in any of them. I would say, "Grandma!" and she would just laugh and rock that much harder. "The boys don't know the meaning of the words," she would say.

She also put brewed highly sweetened coffee into the baby's bottles of milk when she babysat them until I made her stop because it kept them awake at night with nightmares. She made her coffee each morning in a pot on that black wood burning stove by filling the coffeepot with cold water and dumping in several spoons of ground coffee. As the day wore on, she would just add more water and push it to a slightly cooler part of the stove where it would continue brewing the entire day. Sometimes that coffee was so strong by evening it would have grown hair on a lumberjack's chest and she was feeding it to my babies. When pouring a cup you wanted to pour it really slowly so you didn't rile up the grounds down in the bottom. When that happened, you nearly had to sip it through closed teeth to strain out the dregs. The boys loved her to pieces and now enjoy all kinds of coffee concoctions; perhaps that is where they got their love of coffee?

She became so attached to our first son, Lonnie, that when we told her we were expecting a second child, she declared she was not going to get that attached to him. But within six months or so Douglas had her wrapped around his little finger and she was merrily rocking and singing dirty ditties to him also. Mickey had been her favorite grandson and our two sons were her favorite great grandsons.

Before Mickey was born an older sister, Esther Gayle "Pud", was born and Grandma had gotten very attached to her. Lizzie and her friend, Pauline Anthony assisted Lenore at the birth of Mickey. Pauline heard Grandma say she was not going to claim Mickey because she had gotten too attached to Pud, so Pauline said "I will claim him myself." To her dying day, Pauline would call herself Mickey's grandmother and that was OK. You can't have too many grandmas who love you and bake sweets for you.

Pauline and Bert Anthony. Pauline was Mickey's "other" grandmother.

We were living at Stone Head in 1963 when our house burned and we lost almost everything. Pauline invited me to come to her house which was located at the junction of Elkinsville Road and Gravel Creek Road. When I got there she had her collection of kitchen bowls sitting everywhere in the kitchen. The collection covered every available inch of space. She told me to pick any of them I wanted. I finally chose a large white inside, yellow outside bowl, very plain and said that would be just right.

Pauline then told me that I had not done a good enough job picking one out. "Every woman needs something pretty. Now, pick any bowl in this kitchen that you like." I finally chose a red and clear thumbprint bowl. I use it today when I make fruit salad for family dinners and it is lovely and yes, Pauline was right. Every woman needs something pretty. I value that bowl very highly and remember her each time I use it.

Pauline's husband Bert was the son of George Anthony who lived to be 109 years old, and the brother of Cloyd Anthony who lived to be 103.

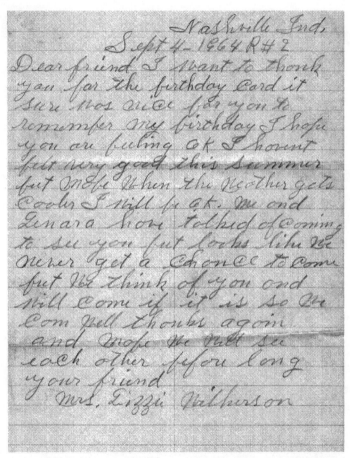

Grandma's handwritten letter to Mrs. Carl Hall.

Grandma was a good letter writer and often exchanged cards and letters with friends. I found one of her hand-written notes to Carl Hall's wife in Elkinsville. A postage stamp for a letter in 1964 was still 5 cents.

Envelope showing the price for a first class stamp in 1964 was 5 cents.

Time passed and Lonnie started attending school. Grandma insisted that he be allowed to get off the school bus at her house each afternoon. After much debate we agreed even though she was getting far along in years by that time. He was in the second grade when she had a mild stroke and had to be admitted to the hospital for a few days. Upon her return home I told her I didn't think she should babysit Lonnie and said we would let him get off next door at Mick's brother Scott's house. This went on about a week before she convinced us to change the way of things. "It is just too cold for him to get off and walk all the way to Scott's house," she explained. To go to Scott's meant he had to walk perhaps 100 feet to go there so there was no chance he would freeze.

What it boiled down to was she missed having him there to eat supper with her each evening. She had always hated eating alone and was tickled to death that he was there every afternoon after school to spend two or three hours with her until we got home from work. She actually ate better herself because of his company so she was healthier. Grandma had this funny habit of never putting more than one kind of food on her plate to eat at a time. When that food was gone, she would place another food on a clean portion of her plate. By the time she and Lonnie had finished eating supper, laughing and talking merrily as he entertained her with stories from school—he was a real jabberwocky—she would have eaten quite a bit of food. Each day she would cook his favorite foods, bake him pies, cakes or other goodies and look forward to her conversations with him. They truly loved each other greatly. We finally relented and let them be together as long as she was able to watch him properly. Douglas was still too young to attend school at this time, so he was at a different babysitter's house.

Grandma Lizzie, the granny woman of our family, had a homemade cure for everything. For instance, a scraping from a raw white potato, applied to the closed eye and bandaged, will remove eye pain immediately. A piece of raw fat meat placed over a splinter or briar embedded under the skin and bandaged will pull the barb from the skin almost overnight. Green tobacco soaked in kerosene and wrapped loosely around a thorn is said to do the same thing. Plain flour browned in a skillet makes an ideal cure for diaper rash on babies. I used this a lot because my kids were allergic to talcum powder.

There were many of these "cures" in Grandma Lizzie's repertoire if you lived over them. Dosing with castor oil was another of her favorite antidotes for any ailment. Castor oil must have been a miracle cure-all for all old women. All of them dosed their children regularly with this vile stuff.

One of the funniest things I can remember about Grandma was her advice to me about a problem I encountered. I had started working at a job corps center that was housed inside an old World

War II army hospital. Evidently I and four other women in the same building picked up the same staph germ since we all came down with the same problem in a short period of time.

We got some very painful cysts in a very private part of our anatomy. This is like an abscess that swells the gland enormously and is so extremely painful it becomes unbearable. When you have one that is active you are in excruciating agony and surgery is the only answer but I did not know that with this first one.

The first time I had one—I had 13 of them in all and the other women each had several apiece—Grandma Lizzie told me to mix softened bacon grease with chimney soot and smear this on the cyst and it would open and drain. She even mixed some up for me herself and sent it via Mickey in one of those old fashioned glass lined zinc can lids.

Anxious for relief I took her at her word and tried this, figuring what could it hurt to try her "cure." At that point in time in my agony I would have tried anything and did so but I would learn very quickly to regret listening to her.

The only problem with Grandma's cure was it did not work as swiftly as I desired. I decided to see a "real" doctor but found out prior to seeing him that the area was too sore to scrub; I could not get this black, greasy concoction off my body.

Desperate for relief, I went on in to see him anyway. When I undressed and was being examined while totally vulnerable, the doctor asked me what the black greasy mess was and I explained about Grandma Lizzie's cure.

He began laughing so hard the tears were rolling down his face and he had to get a chair and sit down across the room from me. Every time he looked my way, the uncontrollable laughter began again. When he was able to quit laughing enough to concentrate on my problem he took care of it by numbing the offending part. Once it was numb, he had his nurse—who was also having laughing fits—wash the black gooey substance off.

That was my last visit to his office. I was too embarrassed to ever see him again. If he is still alive I'll bet he still occasionally laughs when he thinks of my predicament. I know he would have never forgotten Grandma's cure and the resulting black mess.

We visited Grandma Lizzie one evening and I realized she had had another stroke. She was admitted to the hospital again and died a couple of days later. I was the last person to give her a bath, feed her her supper and brush and loosely braid her hair. She thanked me for my attentions and as Mickey and I left her hospital room, she told us bye then closed her eyes and never woke up.

Grandma Lizzie is still spoken of fondly by the many grand- and great-grandchildren who knew her. She is buried in Mt. Zion Cemetery east of Story next to her husband Grover.

Icel and Chloe Carmichael

Icel Carmichael was another resident of the Story community whose humor and antics were very much appreciated by almost all who knew him. He lived with his wife, Chloe, in the big two-story farmhouse on the hill overlooking the Story General Store and next door to Brunell and Ralph Hedrick. They had a black spaniel type dog named "Timmy" that hated most people and me in particular.

Their house was almost directly across the road from Grandma Lizzie's house but she did not appreciate him as much as some of us did. Icel and Grandma were always feuding about one thing or another, none of which amounted to much, but irritated the other person no end. This feuding had become almost a habit with both of them over the years.

Sometimes Grandma would see him out in his field next to her garden plowing the field and accuse him of plowing too close to their fence divider.

"You're ripping up the roots of some of my plants and pulling on my grape arbor," she would yell at him angrily.

Icel would respond by yelling right back at her, "So what, the rain water dripping from your wood shed roof keeps dripping onto my field. It is always too wet for me to work it."

At that time Grandma Lizzie might have picked up a handful of the walnuts which had shaken down from his tree and fell into her yard. Lobbing them at him with all the force she could muster she would fuss and fume for another five minutes while Icel ignored her.

When one looks back at the frivolous things they argued about you might think each enjoyed the feud. Knowing both of them as well as I did, perhaps they did enjoy it.

Icel and Chloe Carmichael in front of their Story home.

Icel's Chloe was a very gentle, quiet and lovely woman while Icel was a fairly large and boisterous man who loved pulling pranks on his friends and neighbors. They had one daughter, Maxine, who was grown and married to Chester "Chet" Fleetwood and had two children before I met Icel and Chloe.

Chloe was a severe diabetic and had to watch everything she ate, but what she couldn't eat Icel and my husband could. That included all manner of fish from nearby Salt Creek and animals from the woods behind his home which abutted the Brown County State Park. The two men were 40 years apart in age but fast friends nevertheless.

Icel and his daughter, Maxine.

For several of his teenage years my husband Mickey lived at his Grandma's house and he became best friends with Icel. The two of them would dig worms and go to the creek together and fish the entire day away. They never caught many "big" fish, but they caught a lot of little sunfish, crappie and bluegill. Occasionally they might even catch a bass or catfish, or in early spring a batch of suckers might be gigged from the creek. None of the fish ever went to waste. The two of them would clean every fish they caught and either Chloe or Grandma would fry them up in a pan of grease which each of the men would then thoroughly enjoy.

This wild game and fish provided a large part of the protein diet needed by the area families in the very desperate days of the Great Depression and during World War II. Most of them had been dirt poor since long before the depression days. It would take a long time for them to become anywhere near prosperous, so "free" meat and fish were always welcome.

Other times the two friends might go squirrel or rabbit hunting together. Both were crack marksmen and they rarely came back from the woods empty handed. Instead they could usually be counted on to dump out on the ground several of the bushy-tailed critters to be cleaned.

They would hold them by the back legs or nail the feet to a tree or the side of a woodshed or something and begin skinning them, being careful to keep as much of the hair off the meat as they possibly could and cleaning any stray shot out of the meat. Chloe or Grandma Lizzie would keep enough fresh squirrels or rabbits to cook tender. Sometimes the women made gravy in the broth and filled it with luscious dumplings. If the squirrels and rabbits were very young and tender, they might be fried right then and the remainder of their kills could be frozen or canned for later meals.

I had been married to Mickey and acquainted with Icel only about three months when Icel found a way to send me into a tailspin. Mickey worked on the night shift at Cummins Engine Co. in Columbus at that time. One night after he left for work it started raining cats and dogs. The rain poured down in absolute torrents for hours on end during the night. I spent the night with Grandma because I was scared of staying alone while he was at work. I had grown up one of eight children and prior to my marriage I had never slept in a bed by myself, much less slept in a house by myself, so I was a real chicken and spent many nights at Grandma Lizzie's.

That same afternoon Mickey had driven his beautiful 1959 fire engine red Chevrolet convertible to Stone Head and met his carpool there. He parked the car on a pull off area from State Road 135 and left it there in front of Laurent Gredy's General Store. Many people parked their cars there then rode in carpools as he did with others, but that night his was the only car in the pull off.

When I awoke the next morning after the rain had stopped I learned from the radio that we had received nearly eight inches of rain the previous night. I looked out the window of Grandma's house and saw a veritable sea of water absolutely roaring everywhere. I had never lived near flood waters and I was petrified.

Her house was about a half mile from Salt Creek but this morning the creek had come almost to her house to greet us when we got out of bed. The roar of the rushing creek was enormous. My own little honeymoon cottage, which was located a couple hundred yards to the south behind Clothie's house, was totally isolated by the rapidly flowing water. I know if I had stayed by myself the previous night and woke up to see the flood water eddying around my house I probably would have died of fright. We had had a beautiful garden just coming into bloom and now you could see none of it. Everything was either washed away or covered by mud and ruined when the water eventually went down. The huge culvert pipe in front of the Story General Store had been all but obliterated. The pipe was still in place, but all the dirt and gravel around the pipe was washed away. It was truly a devastated landscape.

Along in the afternoon when Mickey still had not arrived home from work I became panicky. His brother Scott and I, who were nearly the same age, and by then worried and bored, went together to call on Icel and Chloe.

We plopped down on the couch and Icel sat in his big easy chair. Chloe just kept flitting around bringing us coffee and lemonade. I explained how worried I was about Mickey not being able to get home. Maybe he had been washed away, etc. All I could do was look out their front bow window where the gigantic fern hung suspended in a tub by chains anchored in the ceiling, and try not to cry.

Icel picked up on that right now and started presenting me with all kinds of scenarios that could have happened to Mickey. If I remember correctly Scott went right along with Icel. Icel said they might have been swept into White River near Columbus if they tried to come home by way of State Road 46. "That water gets real high there right this side of the railroad tracks," he told me. I was so young and dumb I didn't know they were teasing.

Chloe could not get the guys to hush but she could see I was truly worried. I can tell you right now I did not appreciate Icel's humor that day. Finally, near dark, Mickey was able to get through the floodwater and come home but his new car was destroyed.

A lovely profile of the gentle Chloe Carmichael.

When he and his carpool buddies ultimately were able to reach Stone Head that afternoon after detouring many times in their efforts to get home safely, they could see about two inches of the convertible's soft top and a tiny bit of the radio antennae with its bedraggled and requisite squirrel tail fluttering just above the swirling muddy water. He wanted to know why I hadn't gone to Stone Head and gotten his car. I was a basket case and had not thought one time about getting Scott to drive me up there to bring it home. I had keys, I had a driver and Grandma's car, but I just had not thought about retrieving it when the rain started. I had not grown up around water so I didn't realize how vast and destructive it could be.

Icel got a big laugh about my jitters and I gave him a bad tongue lashing about making me so nervous with his tales of possible events that could have happened to Mickey. He would just laugh and slap his thigh with his open hand.

Nearly every afternoon after we had the two boys, if I was at home with them, we went for a walk down toward Story just to get some exercise. Both were walking well by that time but Doug would occasionally tire and I would have to carry him.

One day we were walking and had gotten to the place called Sawmill Bank which was located just before we would have come upon Sherman Robertson's place. Our dog, a rat terrier named Chigger, was with us and when he saw this big deer up on the bank above us he started barking fiercely.

When I looked up on that hillside I saw the biggest deer I had every seen in my life. It would have equaled a saddle horse in size and had five or six normal sized does with him; compared to him they were in miniature. The rack on his head was so wide and reached out so far he almost looked like an elk standing there. This thing was huge.

Chigger was determined to save us from this big guy and went tearing up the hillside toward the deer herd. I was petrified that the big buck would jump down off that bank on top of us. If he had there would have been only little wet spots left in the road of us. Chigger did a good job and once he got right up to that big guy, he finally turned and went on up the hill. We were saved.

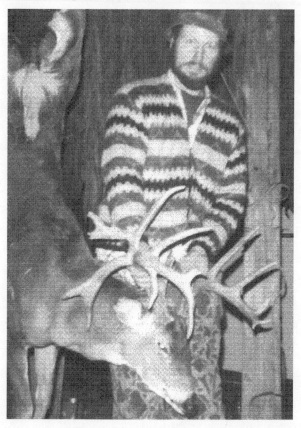

A 21 point buck that was killed by Mickey's cousin Roland Collins. The deer I saw on our walk was much larger than this one.

When I got to the store and told the tale no one would believe I had seen a deer that large. That is no one but Icel believed me. He admitted he had seen a buck this size while hunting up near the park so he could verify its existence at least and said I was not lying about its size. Not many years later another cousin, Aunt Ann's son, Roland Collins, killed a deer with 21 points that was almost, but not quite as large as the one I saw.

One other incident about Icel sticks out in my memory. To me it was the funniest thing I ever heard about him.

One wintry day a light snow had fallen so Icel and Mickey decided they would go deer hunting back near the state park where it touched his own land. The neighborhood men kept three or four conservation officers busy trying to catch them in the act of poaching, but I don't know of a single time they were ever actually caught.

Soon after Mickey and Icel left Icel's house early that fateful morning I was speaking about, they saw a deer and one of them shot it with a .22 caliber rifle, bringing it down. Mickey climbed up a tree and tied a rope over a limb and they hoisted the deer's carcass into the tree and dressed it out right there on the spot. After cleaning the deer, they hoisted it a little higher into the tree and tied it off with the rope to keep predators away from their meat.

Then the other of this Frick and Frack pair said he wanted to kill his own deer so they continued on their way. It wasn't long before they spied another deer and shot it also, but it was able to jump up and bound away from them. They began tracking the deer through the state park because they did not want it to suffer and they wanted the meat. Through that entire long cold day they tracked that deer for miles, reminding each other all the way, "Well, at least we have one back there hanging in that tree if we don't find this one."

It was usual for the guys to use .22 rifles to hunt with. They were all crack shots and the retort from the .22 was usually small enough it would not alert cruising game wardens.

Finally about dark, failing to find the injured deer, they started the long trek home so they could retrieve the one deer left hanging in the tree. The two of them were exhausted and wanted to get home and get something to eat and drink and find a warm place to settle down in for the night.

Scott and I had been almost ready to call someone to help him go look for the hunters when darkness fell and they still were not home. Around 9 p.m. that dark night they finally arrived back home, nearly frozen, hungry as bears and so mad they could hardly explain why they were mad.

After all that walking in the cold and snow and not being able to find the second deer they had shot, Mickey and Icel arrived back at the tree where the first deer had been left only to find the rope hanging limply from the tree, still tied off but minus the deer. Even the hide was gone. "Some dirty rat has stolen our deer," Icel yelled. They both swore vengeance and came into the house.

They were fed, calmed a bit and bedded down for the night. The next morning, lo and behold, there was the deer's hide and head slung across Icel's mailbox. "That has to be Odon who did that," Icel said. Someone was truly asking for retribution for that insulting trick.

Icel Carmichael

Icel and his brother, Odon, had had a falling out several years prior to this time. Odon lived about three hundred yards west of Icel and the two were always after each other to see who could outdo the other with their mean pranks. Icel was convinced until his dying day that his brother had stolen the deer and, to flaunt the deed, had thrown the bloody hide including the head over his mailbox. I was never sure who did the trick but I and many others have laughed about the deed dozens of times over the years.

It was strange that hunting was such a big part of my husband's life in his younger years after what happened in 1968.

He had to have experimental, first of its kind heart surgery, and was not expected to live. While he was in the intensive care isolation ward, he told me, "Helen, I'll never hunt again. That pigeon on my window sill is keeping me alive."

I looked where he indicated and the window was flush with the outside of the building and had no ledges upon which a pigeon could roost.

When Mickey survived and came home he never hunted again and became quite an animal and bird enthusiast instead. He never remembered telling me the tale of the pigeon.

We were living in Stone Head in 1963 when our rental log home caught fire and burned to the ground. Within three days we had a home to live in, free of rent for six months, enough furniture to get by on and enough soft home furnishings for two or three families, all thanks to the generosity of the Van Buren residents we knew.

Knowing we had those two babies, Icel and Chloe bought a home pasteurizer and for six months or so furnished us with all the fresh cow's milk we could use. They had only one milk cow, but they very freely gave nearly everything it produced to my family. This is friendship personified.

They also gave me a new steam iron and ironing board. About once each month for a long time, they would show up at our house with several boxes of dry and canned goods to use at our table. The iron no longer works and I have replaced it, but I am still using that old ironing board when one is needed. Each time I press something on it, I remember Icel and Chloe.

You cannot buy friendships such as was given to us by these two kind people. There is not enough money in the world to buy such happiness, kindness and generosity.

Icel and Chloe Carmichael's home as it looks today.

One evening while I was in night school sharpening my office skills Mickey was babysitting our young sons. He decided to walk with them down to his Grandma's house to watch "Gunsmoke" with her which was her favorite show of all time. We didn't even have a television we were so poor so he enjoyed visiting with Grandma and watching TV with her. He was nearly in Grandma's yard when he heard Chloe start screaming and crying. He quickly handed the boys off to Grandma and ran up the steep yard to see what the problem was. Once Chloe was able to control Timmy the dog, Mickey was able to enter the house.

When Mickey got into their house he found Chloe crying over Icel who had collapsed into his big chair and died in front of her thus ending the story of this legend. They had been to town that day and had just returned and were off-loading their groceries. They had to carry them up their steep yard so he had to sit down to rest. He sat down in his easy chair and died quietly on the spot. It was January 28, 1966, and Icel was 69 years old, (Mickey's age now). Chloe would live several years after Icel passed away. She lived with her daughter Maxine Fleetwood and her husband Chet on State Road 46 until her own death at the age of 78, on October 18, 1979. Both these wonderful people were buried in the Houston Cemetery just across the line in Jackson County from which area Chloe had originally come.

Brunell Hedrick

Brunell Hedrick was the wife of Ralph Hedrick whose family owned the Story General Store for many years. She and Ralph were the parents of one child, a son, Robert or Bob as he was known by all who knew him; and were grandparents to Bob's children Richard, Kathy and Alice Ann. Another son had died in infancy.

Ralph and Brunell Hedrick with their young son, Bob.

Brunell and Ralph lived in a house adjacent to the store between it and the Carmichael homestead. When I moved into the neighborhood Bob was already married to Maxine Kelp and they had three children. Not many years after I met them the elder Hedricks moved from this location in Story to about a mile East on State Road 135 to a farmhouse they owned. It was located next door to Bob's new brick house and across the road from the main part of their farm. A few years later, on October 16, 1972, Ralph, 78, would be killed after a tractor rolled on him and Brunell would become a part of my story of legends.

Bob Hedrick with his school bus for route 39. This
was after he lost a foot in a farm accident.

Strangely enough, both Ralph and his brother Lloyd were injured on their tractors. Lloyd's tractor rolled on him and he lost one leg at the hip as a result but he would live several years after that mishap. Ralph's son, Bob, lost a foot in a farm accident when his pant's leg got caught in a piece of machinery. One would hardly have known

Bob had an artificial foot he got along so well, even driving a school bus and farming for many years after his accident.

Bob died November 16, 1996 at age 69.

Ted Hedrick with his second wife, Kay.

Lloyd's son, Ted, 65, was killed November 16, 1999, when his all terrain vehicle (ATV) overturned on him near Salt Creek. Lloyd's other son, Marvin, 47, a TV antenna installer, died August 26, 1973, after falling from a tower while installing an antenna near Nashville. As you can see, some of the Hedrick men died violent deaths.

I did not know for many years after the fact that Brunell fed my boys whenever they walked by and smelled the aroma of something good cooking or baking at her house.

Our boys grew up in the tidy little house we had built almost adjoining the Brown County State Park in Copperhead Hollow, now named Susie Ayers road, and they used the state park as their playground. They ran over and through the woods and hills like healthy young deer. If they got hungry and it was a "fer piece to home" they were not averse, they tell me, to just stopping by any house along their way home to ask for something to eat or drink. They knew who lived in every house along their route; knew it was safe to stop in; and they knew the women were soft touches so they took advantage of that fact.

The boys were never shy (well, at least Lonnie never was) and they sometimes resorted to slight trickery to get something to eat. If they got hungry they needed food to fuel their active bodies. They might be on the hilltop above Brunell's farmhouse and smell something wonderful cooking or baking in her kitchen. They would run down the hill and make some noise to get her attention so she would know who was outside and not be alarmed.

"Man," Lonnie might say to her (he did most of the talking and begging) "Me and Doug were up on that hill and smelled something wonderful. What are you cooking (or baking)."

Now, Brunell was not stupid—she knew exactly what tricks the boys were up to. She had raised one son and had a grandson. She knew what tricks they could play.

She might have responded, "I am baking brownies and they are just about done. Come inside while I check on them," and the boys would eagerly follow her inside. I can just image the scenario.

A young Lonnie Ayers, wise enough to cadge food from good neighborhood cooks.

A young Douglas Ayers, he let Lonnie do the begging for him.

Lonnie would take a big long drawn out whiff of the air and say, "Man, those things smell good. Are they done yet?"

Brunell would remove them from the oven, drizzle chocolate icing over them and offer to cut them a piece. That offer would be eagerly accepted. Then she probably would have offered them a glass of milk or Kool-Aid or something and this too would be gratefully accepted. After seconds or even thirds their hunger might be slaked enough they could make it the rest of the way home if they hurried. She lived only a mile or so from us but you know how hungry boys can get.

Lonnie was always the biggest eater and largest in size of the two boys. He would eat his brownies quickly and give a big loud burp, and laughing aloud, his eyes alight with mischief, say, "Excuse me." He would then look over at Doug's plate and see that Doug had not yet eaten all of his second helping. Doug ate much slower and ate much less food than Lonnie. Lonnie would ask, "Hey Doug, aren't you going to eat that?" Doug would claim to be full and push the plate to Lonnie who would wolf that treat down too. His appetite was prodigious.

I know those two boys so well I can almost hear them tricking Brunell like this. It was the same if they walked by and she was picking up limbs and twigs from her yard or mowing grass. They would tell her she was working too hard and offer to do the chores for her. She would accept and go inside and get their treats while they finished up her chore.

Every woman up and down the road fell for their tricks and fed my two kids at some time or another over the years. They ate whole meals, cookies, cakes, brownies, turnovers, candy or anything that would have been offered. I didn't know that for many years but I am not at all surprised to hear that it happened. The boys were young, attractive, courteous, and respectful of the older generation (especially if the woman was a good cook) and they were always glad to pay their way by doing little chores.

Many of these lonely widows probably fed them just to hear their boisterous laughter and their talk about their adventures in the woods or along the trails surrounding Salt Creek. I'm sure their house rang with echoes of their enthusiasm long after they had departed. They brightened the days of so many of these wonderful women.

Former President Bill Clinton's wife, Hillary Rodham Clinton, was quoted widely during his presidency as saying it "took a village to raise a child". I can believe that because Brunell was part of our sons' village. While I worked outside the home, the older, gentler women of our neighborhood kept a keen eye on our boys. She died June 27, 1978 a short time before her 76th birthday and is buried in the McKinney Cemetery along with all the other Hedricks I have mentioned above.

The Hedrick Family Photo Album

One of my favorite pictures that Maxine loaned me shows Albert (Pink) Hedrick handing the wood to his son Ralph inside the steam powered tractor. They used this tractor to power their sawmill in Story.

Bob Hedrick as he looked as a soldier.

Susan (Suz) Hedrick with her grandson Richard Hedrick.
Suz is wearing her mop cap and granny apron.

Suz Hedrick and her daughter, Lillie. Notice the dresses they are wearing.

A much younger Ralph and Brunell Hedrick

Bob and Maxine Hedrick in their wedding photo.

A nice family photograph shows seven members of the Hedrick family standing together. From left, they are: Marvin Hedrick, Ted Hedrick, Albert Pruitt, Albert (Pink) Hedrick, his wife, Susan (Suz) Hedrick, Robert (Bob) Hedrick and Alfred Pruitt.

This is a very early photograph of Lloyd and Agnes Hedrick.

This is Marvin Hedrick, the son of Lloyd and Agnes, sitting on a dog's back pretending to ride his horsey maybe when he was a young boy.

The Fleetwood Clan

Winfer may have been his real given name, but I don't recall ever hearing Winfer Fleetwood referred to by anyone as anything other than Bud as long as I knew him.

Bud was one of the three sons of Howard and Sharlot Fleetwood. The sons included Winfer (Bud), Chester (Chet) and Arthur (Art). There also was a daughter, Lucy. The Fleetwood men whom I knew best were Bud and Chet and their wives.

Bud and his wife Mary Louise Ogle Fleetwood and their two children, Jerry and Donita, lived the first house on the left as you went north on Gravel Creek Road. At the time I met them Jerry was a young pre-teen boy and Donita was only three or four years old.

Bud operated an excavating business, hauled gravel, farmed a little and drove a school bus. Mary Louise (I always just called her Louise) kept house and assisted Bud in his various enterprises and was an accomplished seamstress. That family would become dear friends of ours over the next few years. This couple was a little older than my husband and I, but age did not stand in the way of our friendship.

Bud and Louise Fleetwood with their grandson,
Daniel, in 1979. Bud was diagnosed with cancer the
following month and died 13 months later.

Since Gravel Creek was not that far from our house, and if the boys ran through the state park as was their custom, the Fleetwood home was easily on their daily travels. I am sure they made brief "rest" stops at the Fleetwood homestead and cadged some good vittles from Louise. She told me several police and conservation officers had been known to stop for a cup of coffee and a slice of her homemade pies. Word spreads fast in small neighborhoods of which woman is a good cook or baker of goodies. Our boys knew them all.

Most of the women I mention, who lived around the Story community, baked pies or cakes several times each week. You could almost always count on them to have at least part of a pie in the pie safe or refrigerator if you stopped by to visit. You never left their homes without having been offered something to eat or drink. That was just the custom in those parts in that time and place.

Fairly tall and slim as a rail slat, Bud had almost platinum blond curly hair and the biggest 100 watt smile I ever saw. He never met a stranger nor many people he didn't like. He was also just one of the best looking men I had ever seen. Ladies, he was one mmmmm-mmm-mm-good looking man. He was a Chippendale before that term was coined. I may have been married but I was not totally blind the first time I saw this sun-browned tightly-muscled Adonis smiling radiantly at me from his seat on a bulldozer in my front yard.

Over the years Bud would do quite a bit of excavating for us and he hauled many loads of gravel to our various home sites and hauled our boys to school for many years.

Their house was an older white farmhouse in excellent condition, shaded by three or four huge stately maple trees. It sat about a tenth of a mile off Gravel Creek Road and across the small creek for which the road was named, next to the west hillside. It was a lovely spot for a house with its big old-fashioned wooden barn and its green lawn sloping down toward the little creek. The scene, when fall wore its splendid colors, would have put a Norman Rockwell painting to shame.

Bud and Louise's home was about a half mile away north of his mother and father, Howard and Sharlot Fleetwood. Their home was located about a quarter of a mile west on Elkinsville road from the turnoff onto Gavel Creek Road.

During the Great Depression there was very little means of earning a living in Brown County. The elder Fleetwoods decided to follow the example of several of their neighbors who had migrated to the rich farmlands in Illinois. There in Grand Ridge, Illinois, they became sharecropper farmers and would stay through the birth of their children.

The whole Fleetwood clan, from left; Winfer, Lucy,
Arthur, Chester, Sharlot and Howard.

According to Maxine Fleetwood, the widow of Chester, times became very lean here in Brown County and Sharlot's parents, Isom and Sally Arwine Wilkerson, were in danger of losing their homestead. They begged Howard and Sharlot to return and take over the operation of their farm, which they did, rearing their children in the farmhouse now occupied by their grandson, Ron Fleetwood. Ron has served as the Brown County Superintendent of Highways for several years now.

Ron Fleetwood is the Brown County Highway Superintendent today.

Maxine said, "I'm glad for the way things turned out or I would not have met Chester." He had only to walk up the road about a mile and a half to court her as was the common custom in those days. Without having transportation, you looked close to home for a pretty girl.

I don't recall that Bud ever kept livestock other than a few chickens but maybe at some time or other he had done so and I was just not aware of it or have now forgotten.

*Chester and Maxine Carmichael Fleetwood
during his stint in the U. S. Navy.*

He was the school bus driver for many years for our sons and they had an excellent rapport with Bud. Bud appreciated Doug's various artistic talents and tenacity and was always challenging him. Lonnie's get-rich-quick schemes amused Bud greatly and Bud was always interested in hearing Lonnie's latest plan.

The boys tell me that Bud was a trickster of sorts. When driving them to school he had to pass by Rex Kritzer's pig lot which abutted State Road 135 just before you got to Stone Head. In warm weather, the stench from this h-o-g pig lot stunk so badly the kids on the bus would roll the windows up and hold their breath until the bus passed it by. I said h-o-g pig because my husband and others make fun of the way I pronounce the word hog. They tell me I say, h-a-a-a-a-g, kind of gushing it out like a southern belle, so now I just say h-o-g pig.

There was a big hump in the highway right where the pigs were located. "The kids would all get quiet when we passed the Kritzer's house," Doug told me. "We were all holding our breath and couldn't talk the stink was so bad."

Bud had previously noticed how quiet the kids got when he came to the Kritzer hog lot so he would slow way, way down and take as long as possible to get past the odor.

Finally, just when the kids were turning blue from holding their breaths so long Bud would laugh heartily, speed up and go over the hump and down into the following deep dip and nearly bust their heads on the roof of the bus. They had to hang onto their seats to stay in place when he raced down the yon side of the dip and started up the other side. There were two humps like this along their route so every day was like riding a small roller coaster.

Bud took what could have been a boring trip to school and made it fun and exciting for the kids on his bus. As each kid got on the bus it was greeted the same way by Bud, "Get that hair out of your eyes," he would demand. Every kid on that bus thought the world of him.

The other thing he did which still rattles around in the boy's heads was play eight-track Statler Brothers and Alabama tapes over and over along their way to school. Those same two tapes were played during the entire school year they tell me until even today the songs replay over and over in their heads when things get quiet.

One day Bud asked Mickey to come to his house and assist him with a machinery repair chore of some kind. Mickey took Douglas, who was about nine at the time, with him when he went because Doug enjoyed visiting Bud so much.

When they got there Doug saw a flock of bantam chickens and roosters strutting and running around Bud's yard, scratching at bits of gravel and pulling worms and bugs from the lawn.

Doug, like any energetic boy, tried to catch the chickens by chasing them but if you have ever seen a banty chicken run you know how fast and elusive they can be. They may be small, but man they are fast. Doug couldn't catch them no matter how fast he ran. Finally giving up his chase, sweaty and exhausted, he flopped down in the grass on his back to rest.

Bud saw what he was trying to do and jokingly threw him a challenge. "Doug," he said, "If you can catch those chickens I'll let you take home however many you catch."

These words from Bud were like a gauntlet thrown before Doug and Bud knew he would not be able to resist the challenge. Mickey and Bud then went about their business, leaving Douglas to play in the yard.

Doug sat and pondered the problem for a while before he thought of a solution. Once he thought he had the problem solved, he quietly walked into the big wooden barn and searched around until he found several gunny sacks that had been left lying about. Taking them outside he tossed most of them in the back of our pickup truck and took one to the small creek that bisected Bud's farm. There he wet the gunny sack thoroughly and sauntered back into the yard with it hanging dripping wet from his hand.

Laying the wet sack on the ground, he then went to his dad and asked to borrow his pocket knife.

"Be careful with that, it is sharp," Mickey told him as he handed a folded pocket knife to Doug. Mick would never hand you an open knife nor accept an open one back from you.

"It's bad luck," he would say. The old timers all thought a knife was bad luck. If they gave you one, like when our house burned, each one I received had a penny taped to it for good luck.

Doug picked up his wet sack and nonchalantly approached a clutch of those banties so as not to alert them, and then quickly threw the now-heavy wet gunny sack over the entire batch. The water made the sack heavy and he could trap them to the ground and retrieve them from under the sack one at a time and place them in a dry sack in which he had by now cut several small holes with the borrowed pocket knife.

The chickens could stick their heads through the holes to get air but they could not get their bodies out. Chickens truly must be pretty stupid because the remainder of the flock never caught on to his tricks and would quickly regroup in bunches after each toss of the wet sack. Doug could then trap and capture another batch.

By the time Mickey was ready to leave, Doug's job was complete. He had crawled inside the pickup to rest and wait for his dad.

Bud leaned inside and said, "Hey, Doug how many chickens did you catch?" He was probably remembering how Doug had been chasing them earlier and not being successful.

"Every single solitary one of them. Look in the back of the truck," Doug told Bud as a huge grin lighted his young face.

Chagrined, Mickey and Bud looked in the back of our pickup and sure enough there were 21 chickens sticking their heads through the holes he had cut in the sacks. The two men fell against the truck they were laughing so hard.

But true to his word Bud let Doug bring all the chickens home with him. For awhile we had banty roosters crowing from the rooftops and colorful hens roosting in the trees in the yard until finally they were so old they died or predators had caught them. It would be the only time in our married life that we would be in the chicken business, thanks to Bud Fleetwood. I have often wondered if Bud regretted making that deal with a little boy, but knowing him, I would bet he got a kick out of the story every time he told it. Nobody liked a good tale better than Bud.

Our house was located not quite far enough off the main highway for Bud's school bus to have to drive to pick the boys up, but Mick's cousin Danny was still in school and lived on up dead end Copperhead Hollow from us. At that time we were the only two families on Susie Ayers Road. Since Danny qualified for pickup because of distance, Bud would pick our kids up too. When Danny got old enough to drive a car to school, Bud made deals with our kids. On the non-rainy days if they would walk down to the highway and meet the bus there he would pay them $15 each semester. That was like giving them candy and they grabbed that deal. It worked well for both Bud and the boys. The boys didn't mind walking the few hundred feet home at night or to the bus in the mornings, and Bud didn't have to maneuver his long school bus up that narrow lane.

Mickey would often fill in whenever either Bud or Chester needed an extra hand in their businesses. Chester worked at Cummins Engine Company in Columbus until his retirement and he also owned a bulldozing outfit. He was chosen to serve as the president of the Diesel Worker's Union for many years. Mickey and Chet's son, Ron, worked together on the dozer, creating a lot of memories among them. The two of them were always pulling some kind of trick or another on Chet.

One day Mickey's job was to return the big flatbed trailer, which was normally used to transport the bulldozer, from Gravel Creek to Chet's home on State Road 46 East toward Gnaw Bone. As he traveled along he noticed how everyone was looking at him and laughing. When he got to Chet's place he discovered that our little dog, Chigger, had ridden along on the back of the trailer all that way. Those laughing must have thought it took a mighty big trailer to haul that one little dog.

In June 1979 Bud began feeling sick and was diagnosed with lung cancer. If you have ever known anyone who had lung cancer, then you know how much he suffered. Then they discovered he also had inoperable brain cancer. The prognosis was grim and his treatment harsh.

One day Mickey and I were talking about Bud, wondering how he was getting along with his cancer treatments. I told Mickey I was going to drive over there and see how he was doing. He said for me to go ahead by myself that he didn't think he could bear to see Bud like this.

When I arrived Bud and Louise had just returned from the doctor's office where Bud had had another dose of chemotherapy. I was absolutely shocked when I saw him. In the short time it had been since I had last seen this vital active man, this insidious disease had reduced him to a quivering mass of pain. He was so weakened he almost had to be tied to his kitchen chair for support.

He was now skinny to the point of emaciation. Louise had tried her best to build him up so he could better stand the only known possible help for this disease, chemotherapy. She had made him a nutritious milkshake with all the nutrients he needed just before I got there. She sat it in front of him and placed a bent straw into the glass so Bud could drink.

This wonderful man who had been our friend for so long was so weakened he could no longer grip, lift and hold a glass in his hand; he had to lean forward to drink from the straw. He was barely able to exert enough energy to suck the liquid through the straw.

"Don't feel sorry for me, Helen, I'll be OK," he told me. As sick as he was he tried to cheer me and that just made the thought of losing this friend even more difficult.

That was the last time I saw him alive. I cried all the way home and told Mickey I didn't think he would or could live long. He didn't. He died at age 55, in August 1980 exactly 13 months to the day after his cancer was diagnosed. He was interred in the Christiansburg cemetery beneath a gravestone on which is etched a picture of a bulldozer. Bud truly was a good family man and wonderful friend to all who knew him.

Although Bud died relatively young, his parents, Howard and Sharlot Fleetwood each would live to the great age of 92.

When I ran for county commissioner in the election in 1976, Howard and Sharlot were pretty much confined to their home so the county election board sent a representative from both political parties to their home so they could vote an absentee ballot.

When the election board asked them who they wanted to vote for for the position of county commissioner they both told them they wanted to vote for me.

Howard once told me "They tried every way they knew how to make me change my mind and vote for the party's man. I kept telling them I was voting for you and to mark my ballot that way or leave me alone."

Both the Fleetwoods finally had to get mad and demand that they cast those two votes for me. This was true loyalty. The same thing happened at Lloyd Hedrick's home. I won nearly all the votes in this precinct that year thanks to people like the Fleetwoods and the Hedricks.

Howard died April 24, 1984 and Sharlot died December 17, 1988 long after their son had died. Both the elder Fleetwoods had been friends of ours and Mickey had helped Howard remodel his home. This entire group of Fleetwoods is buried in Christiansburg Cemetery.

Patty Fleetwood, daughter of Chester and Maxine Fleetwood.

*Donita Potts and Jerry Fleetwood, children of
Bud and Mary Louise Fleetwood.*

Bernard *(Bud)* and Eva Brand

As one left the Story community heading West on Elkinsville Road the first house on the right that you came to was the small home of Bud and Eva Brand, their sons Michael and Stephen and their daughter Susan, who was the shyest person I ever met.

They later renovated a large farmhouse just south of Story on State Road 135 which had previously belonged to Howard "Babe" Carmichael, and they still live there. Nowadays there are a couple of new homes in between Story and their old home which they sold several years ago, but at that time, theirs was the first house you came upon.

A very young and beautiful Eva Thompson Brand.

A very young and dapper Bud Brand.

The Brands' sons were each almost exactly a year older than each of our sons. Since these four boys were the only males around in that age group and they lived only about two miles apart, the boys became fast friends at a young age. Their friendship would last a lifetime. Although Michael was older than Lonnie by one year, they were in the same grade of school because Lonnie got to start school at age 5. Stephen and Lonnie were the same age, Doug two years younger. Susan was much younger than the four boys.

Michael Brand as a Green Beret.   *Stephen Brand*   *Susan Brand*

The four boys would share many good times together over the years and entertain both sets of parents a good deal. When Susan was very young, Eva told me to remember where I bought Douglas' clothing because little Susan always wanted a "Doug Ayers T-shirt." I guess Doug was her idol for a while.

Bud and Eva did a lot of farming so she was home every day while I worked away from home. During Little League baseball season each spring Eva and I worked out a system of transporting the boys. Eva would drive the boys to practice and games and leave them at the school. When I got off work I would stop by the school, watch them finish playing, then take them to Nashville for Dairy Queen treats then drop the Brand boys back off at their home. This freed Eva to help on the farm and freed me from having to make special arrangements to get the boys to a ball diamond. The boys would chatter like magpies the entire time they were in the car together.

If I could not make it to pick them up due to job constraints I would call Eva and she would again make the run to the school, DQ and back home. Between us we kept the DQ operating profitably. It is no longer in business—I wonder why?

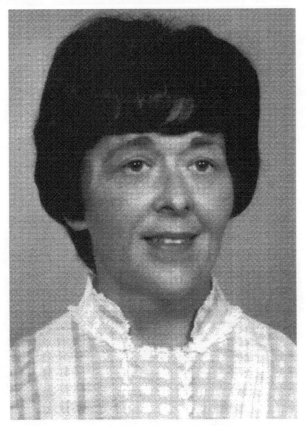

Eva Brand as she looked when I met her.

Eva and I were kind of like the tortoise and the hare. I always drove swiftly but safely. Eva was just the opposite—driving very slowly and safely. All four boys teased her about driving so slowly but their taunts never made her go any faster. Perhaps she got her slow driving habit from her father-in-law, Hiram Brand.

Hiram, a school teacher for 49 years, and his wife, Rosa, lived just west of Pikes Peak on Bellsville Pike. He drove so slowly everyone meeting him could tell within a second of coming up behind him that it was Hiram driving. He had other driving habits such as driving over the humps in the roads partially in the other lane. Hiram scared many of us with that habit. His comment was, "You guys know it is me, you watch out for me." And so we did.

This is a picture of the students in the New Bellsville School in the 1933-34 school year. Kenneth Carmichael was the teacher. Bud Brand, who loaned me this picture, is the second boy from the right in the front row. Bud went on to become a school teacher and taught for 34 ½ years.

During a summer break from high school the four boys, along with a couple of their other friends, decided to make a canoe trip from

Nashville on that branch of Salt Creek, across the Monroe Reservoir and return to Story up that branch of Salt Creek. Two boys were in charge of renting and moving the canoes into position at Nashville; two would buy sufficient food and water supplies; the other two would take care of the tents and other personal supplies such as clothing. Every scrap of food was listed and inventoried and secured in one of the canoes. Each boy was allotted just so much food and water each day so they had to have enough to make it last.

On launch day the canoe handlers brought the canoes to Salt Creek, just behind the Little Nashville Opry, put them into the water and they were off. I think Bud Brand provided the truck for the drop off then drove it back home.

They had an exciting very eventful time during the three day trip, but found out that canoeing on Salt Creek was difficult because there were so many log jams in the creek. They had to do a lot of portaging of those heavily loaded canoes. But once they actually got to the big waters of the reservoir, they had a little easier time.

At one point in their journey someone tipped the canoe which held their tents and clothing, getting everything wet. They could not even start a fire to dry the items because their matches had also gotten wet. They solved this problem by having Lonnie and his crewmate canoe to one of the two stores along State Road 446 near Bloomington.

When they got there they found they had not a penny of money between them and they needed a little more than matches for the remainder of the trip. The proprietor finally said he would spot them some supplies if they could leave something with him as collateral. I guess their honest faces convinced him he could trust the boys. Lonnie, always thinking quickly, discovered he had his pilot's license in his wallet so that was left with the store's owner until he could return and collect it and pay cash for their badly needed supplies. They sure did not relish aborting their canoe adventure and having to have someone come pick them up that far from their destination.

After that things went pretty smoothly and they arrived back almost on time near the Brand farm where the truck to haul the canoes back to the supplier was waiting. They were weary and very tired but they had had a marvelous adventure and would talk about it for a long time.

Lonnie's pilot's license would hold him in good stead another time. He had started taking flying lessons when he was 15 and obtained his pilot's license a short time before he graduated high school.

He and three of his graduating buddies, including Michael, decided they would pool their resources, rent a four-seater plane and Lonnie would fly them all to Chicago for a wild weekend. Everything went as planned and they landed at Midway Airport in Chicago on Saturday about noon. The four boys spent a wonderful weekend in the Windy City then flew home, landing safely in Seymour's Freeman Field.

While they were gone the father of one of the boys called my house looking for his son and I advised him the four of them were in Chicago. His son, another boy also named Michael Brand, (no relation to the first Michael Brand) had told him they were going but the father did not believe him until I confirmed it.

Although Stephen was the third from oldest of this quartet of boys, he married first and had a daughter, Cassie. He and his wife divorced when Cassie was quite young and Steve ran into some personal tribulations as he adjusted to losing his wife and child. Working at it constantly and with the loving support of his family, he had turned his life back around, holding a good job and was doing well.

Steve rode a mo-ped to his job near Columbus each evening. On his last day of life, October 3, 1990, his mo-ped was struck from behind by a vehicle and young Steve, 29, was killed instantly. Our boys, Michael and his sister and his parents were devastated. We missed his funny presence greatly. Steve was kind of quiet at times but he had a marvelous sense of humor at other times. Steve's daughter is now married with a son so his spirit lives on. Had he lived, he would have been 45 today, the same age as our son, Lonnie.

The other three boys each married. Douglas had one son who died on Good Friday, 2004, in Tokyo, Japan where his family resided. His son, George, 11, had been an invalid almost from birth. Lonnie and his wife Conchita, has a son and a daughter and they live in Barcelona, Spain. Michael married a southern girl named Claudia, but they have no children. They now reside in Maryland. Young Susan still lives at home with her sometimes ailing parents. We still call but visits are rare however we feel comfortable with our friendship to this day.

Cassie Brand with her 7 ½ month old son,
Steven. Her father was Stephen Brand.

Bud, a retired school teacher (he taught 34 ½ years) and farmer, has had five hip and knee surgeries along with open heart surgery and gets around on crutches. He is a delight to talk with and enjoys hearing from his friends. Even though he is now 82 years young, he can look at a photograph of his first grade classmates at the Bellsville school and name almost every one of them.

He talked last week about the ways the schools of yore raised funds for the extras that were not included in the school's meager budgets. He remembers how they would have two-day fairs at the school during which they would play games of chance. Any monies raised went directly to the school funds to improve it.

He recalled the cake walks and pie socials that were held during these fairs; someone would knock out partial tunes on an old tinny sounding piano for the cakewalks which people paid a small fee to enter. The pies were auctioned to the highest bidder and the successful bidder got to sit and eat a slice with the one who baked it. They floated a saucer in a pan of water and let people pitch pennies to win a small inexpensive prize; the fish ponds behind curtains where a tiny prize would be attached to your "fishing poles." They would set up quart jars and players would try to toss table tennis balls into the jars and many other games for raising funds. "It was all in fun," he said, "But it was a major fundraising effort."

Bud keeps remembering things he wants to share with me. One was his experience during World War II. He called last week and told me, "I was shipped to Europe on the Queen Mary which had been refitted to be a troop ship and it was quite posh. The ocean was calm and we had an easy crossing."

While he was stationed in Europe he was a member of a 240 millimeter howitzer gun crew. "We had to stay back from our target at least six miles or we would overshoot the target.

"That gun, with its 400 pound projectile was accurate up to a range of eighteen miles," he said.

"It was an awful time for all of us. Sometimes I think it was the shared experiences, the camaraderie, that allowed us to pull through," Bud said.

His return trip to the states, though, after the Battle of the Bulge and numerous other battles, was made in a "tub of a ship" and the ocean was kicking up forty foot waves. He nearly made me seasick telling about how everyone was seasick aboard ship.

"I thought I would die myself for two days," he said. "Then I decided to get up, no matter how rotten I felt, take a shower and shave, and go up on an outer deck." He said he was never seasick after that and recommends it as a way to lessen seasickness.

Eva just never changes. She is ageless and still drives really slowly when she drives at all, while I still putt-putt along at a good rate of speed. Eva is having problems now with macular degeneration so her driving days may soon be behind her.

And now, one final story about Eva's family. Her half brother, Vernal Pruitt, lives near Freetown and we have been acquainted for several years. Vernal is hard of hearing and his wife, Ruby, has visual problems, and Vernal loves to squirrel hunt. When he goes hunting nowadays he takes Ruby with him.

"When she hears a squirrel chattering, she points in the general direction she hears it, and I look in that direction and shoot it."

I'll bet they make a pretty good hunting team. I would surely love to watch this team in action out in the woods.

A recent snapshot of Vernal and Ruby Pruitt.

Vernal recently underwent heart by-pass surgery so I don't want to tease him too much. He raises a really pretty garden most years when he feels like doing the work and he always makes sure I get a couple of messes of fresh green beans.

When I stopped by to take their picture I said to him, "I heard you had been sick?"

"No," he said.

"A little puny?" I queried.

"No." he answered

"Well, did you or did you not have heart by-pass surgery just recently?" I asked.

"Oh, yeah," he answered, "But they only did quadruple by-pass."

So much for my thinking it might have slowed him down a little, and what a wonderful attitude he had to this major event in his 70-year life. Ruby at 74, and Vernal had been stacking wood and both appeared to be hale and hearty.

There are lots of legends in this one little family.

Ansel Hillenburg

We were lucky in having so many nice neighbors, but not every single neighbor can be classified as nice. Some are just down-right devils in disguise. Ansel crawled into our midst one spring upon his release from the state's penal farm system like a snake into my own Eden.

He was the uncle of our landlord so we could not object too strenuously when he was moved into a small trailer/camper next to our driveway which was across the road from where we were renting an old farmhouse.

Although fairly harmless as it would turn out, this WWII veteran, who had not seen a sober day since the end of the war, could be extremely annoying.

His presence in our neighborhood would bring to an end my idealistic existence. Having grown up in a family of non-drinkers and having lived around so many wonderful other members of the neighborhood I was not prepared for Ansel. I had never seen a "wino" in my life.

Ansel was in his late 50's when we were introduced and had not had a bath in recent history. His favorite drink for breakfast, lunch and dinner was not coffee, but a bottle of the cheapest wine he could find for sale on the market. His drink of choice was Gibson's White Port wine with a picture of a pheasant on the bottle's label.

He dressed each day in an old pair of faded blue bibbed overalls with the side buttons undone and a dirty gray sweatshirt. He always seemed to emit this almost gray silhouette or aura about himself, like he was just fading out, not just his clothing, but his body as well. About once each week he might make an ineffective stab at scraping off some of the gray stubble that covered his face. As far as brushing his teeth, that would not happen in his lifetime and were as yellowed as a squirrel's teeth. In other words, this man was dirty and he stank to high heaven. It was best to stay upwind of Ansel.

Mickey has always had a soft spot for veterans and went out of his way to watch out for and help them. His dad, Donald, and an uncle, Clifford, were WWII veterans who had seen a lot of action, so when he was able to do so, he helped old veterans when he could. This practice would continue his entire life. He himself would serve 23 years in the Indiana National Guard. Our son Lonnie served just over fourteen years in the Air Force, entering as an enlisted man and ending up a captain.

The first day that Ansel was ensconced on our rented premises by his niece Sheila Lucas, who was our landlady, was a real eye-opener for me. The house we rented was large, but contained no indoor plumbing. Ansel would share our outdoor toilet which was located at the edge of our lawn, Sheila told us. This would create some problems but they were solvable.

Sheila and her husband, Jack, had bought the farm a year or so prior to our arrival. They actually lived in Gnaw Bone and drove to the farm to do their chores and look after their cows after their jobs were finished in Bloomington. They had plans to remove the old farmhouse and build a big brick house in its place in the future. In the meantime they rented it to us and then later after we had moved, they rented it to the Herschell and Gracie Reed family.

The Reeds would have no problem with Ansel, but I sure would have.

Lonnie (R) and Ansel, 1974, drilling a well on Salt Creek Road.

I had taken one look at this detestable person and made my mind up that I would not like him. That never really changed, but I did feel sorry for him at times.

He had a habit of strolling across the lawn toward the toilet and while doing so he would stop, stand for long periods of time staring all around, especially if I was at home alone with the boys who were quite young at the time. Our little rat terrier dog, Chigger, had no more use for him than I did and would bark crazily at him every time he stepped into the yard. Ansel hated that dog with a passion and kept telling us to get rid of him. We refused, but one day we woke up and the dog was gone, never to be seen again. I always suspected he had killed the dog and buried it, but I never had any proof.

One evening late, not long after Ansel arrived, I had tucked the boys into bed and was sitting on the bed reading them a bedtime story. I began hearing something scraping against the window screen next to their beds. The window was propped open so the air could circulate and it sounded like a small twig was being brushed back and forth across the screen. There was a fairly large flowering shrub about five feet away from the side of the house and I thought it might be that bush moving back and forth in the breeze so I thought nothing of it.

About that time Douglas decided he needed to urinate before he went to sleep. I told him to step outside on the side porch and do his business from there. He went outside, immediately ran back inside, slammed and locked the door then jumped back into bed, quickly pulling the blanket up to his neck like he was hiding.

"There is a man standing out there, Mom," he shakily told me.

I went into the living room and made sure the door had gotten locked then went to a cabinet to retrieve a 12-gauge pump shotgun Mickey kept there. I took a couple of shells from the box and loaded them into the gun's chamber.

Returning to the bedroom I said, loud enough for whoever it was out there to hear me, "Just put your leg over that windowsill and I will blow your behind to Kingdom Come."

On those words I closed the shells in the chamber with a snick, snick and jammed that pump mechanism back and forth to make it ready for firing. It made a very distinct, never to be mistaken for another sound, when the gun was loaded and pumped. Every country person recognizes it instantly. The only response I heard was the sound of heavy booted feet running away from the house.

No longer was I the frightened, naïve young woman I had been when I married. I was now a Mama Bear with two cubs and I would have fought to the death for those cubs. Hear me roar!!!

After the incident was all over I realized I had only fired that shotgun one time in my life. When we were newlyweds Mickey had loaded it for me and told me to hold it down by my side to shoot it. He was afraid if I held it to my shoulder it would kick up and break my jaw or my glasses or bruise my shoulder badly.

"It kicks back pretty hard," I remember he told me.

"Pretty hard" was sure an understatement. I held it to my side as he said and fired that gun down across a field near Story and it picked me up bodily, moved me backwards about three feet and knocked me on my fanny with a hard thud. That ended my wanting to shoot a shotgun of any gauge. But I would have shot it again that night.

But if I had I might have shot one of my kids when it recoiled so I guess it was just as well I didn't have to fire it.

The next morning when Mickey arrived home after working the third shift at Reliance Electric in Columbus, Ansel met him at the driveway and told him, "Ask Helen if she heard someone outside the house last night."

"I saw some tracks out there when I went to the toilet and followed them all the way to the barnyard gate, but lost them," he told Mick.

When I was told what he had said I made up my mind the boys would not go outside at night anymore and I would not share a toilet with this old wino.

From that time on the boys and I used a chamber pot I had found in the slightly leaning storage building which sat next to the toilet. I'm sure it had belonged to the farm's former owners Judd and Eathel Bradley but it was now mine.

This white enamel pot had a white lid with a red ring around the edge of the lid. The night's contents would be dumped into the toilet each morning, rinsed and aired during the day.

Nowadays they call these serviceable containers antiques and use them to hold potted plants and flowers. They always sat within reach under a person's bed at night when I was growing up, and some of them were decorated very prettily with flowers and leaves both inside and out, but no amount of decorating could disguise their intended usage.

I know in my heart it was Ansel outside our bedroom that night. But, being the country person he was, he too knew what the sounds of a pump shotgun being loaded sounded like and that never happened again.

Ansel told us tales about spending each winter in warm cozy quarters, compliments of the State of Indiana. His only real vice was drinking; I never knew him to do anything illegal. But if winter was just around the corner and he had no place to snug down for the coming months, he would ensure that the state did not overlook him when assigning bed space.

He knew if he got arrested often enough for public intoxication, the authorities would take care of him long enough to get through a cold winter. It was not difficult when inside the penal system to get access to cheap booze so he could comfortably spend three months behind bars. For small favors, the guards would look the other way when he received his white port wine.

He once related how one cold fall day he had walked into the jail in Columbus and demanded they lock him up. He was ready to go back to his favorite haunt but the officer on duty said they could not lock him up because he had not done anything wrong.

Ansel told the duty officer, "That's OK," and went outside.

He was cold and determined they were going to give him a bed for the coming winter. Once he was outside he found a good sized stone, returned to the jail and threw the stone through the window. A deputy came outside and escorted Ansel to a cell and he got his customary three-month assignment to the state farm.

I once saw this same scene enacted on the Andy Griffith show when Ernest T. Bass did the same thing. I don't know if Ansel's tale was true or if he too had seen this same show. I do know for a fact that he spent several winters warm and cozy courtesy of the Indiana Penal System.

We eventually completed building our home in Copperhead Hollow and moved there. It was only about a quarter of a mile away, but I felt safer just being away from Ansel; however, he would visit us several times and actually stay in our basement during one cold winter.

Mickey would occasionally take Ansel to work with him. He wasn't much help on our drilling rig, but he was company for Mick. It gave Mickey someone to talk to during the day and made the time pass faster.

Ansel was with him one day while Mickey was drilling a well for the "hippies" near Needmore. The hippies had moved into that area in force some time previously and we had drilled several water wells for them. They were mostly from fairly wealthy families in cities who had decided to drop out and live this primitive lifestyle. Determined to be self sufficient, they were high most of the time on marijuana, but they bought into the culture of exotic animals, chickens, geese, and other types of game. They were going to become "children of the earth."

I'm sure their parents were more than grateful to see them living in this location. At least they were not hanging out in their own basements, smoking pot and doing other things they could have been arrested for. Most of these young people were college educated and could have lived anywhere and probably have been successful. Instead they came to Needmore in far northwestern Brown County, settled in and set up a colony.

Anyway, one day Ansel was with Mickey and needed to urinate. He walked around the side of a big wooden barn, then he came racing back to Mick hollering and grabbing onto Mick with one hand trying to pull him away from the rig, "Come here, Mick, see if you see a buffalo too."

Ansel was coming down off a toot and had had DT's so many times I am sure he thought he was seeing imaginary buffalos instead of pink elephants.

Mickey had been there several times and knew the hippies maintained a small herd of the huge animals. He got a good laugh at Ansel's expense that day and would remind him of it several times in ensuing years.

"Ansel, there is no way you are seeing a buffalo. I have been here a dozen times and I haven't seen one yet," Mick told him and just kept the drilling machine going.

Ansel pulled on his arm demanding, "Turn that thing off or shut it down and come and look," he begged.

Finally, Mick consented and walked behind the barn with the old sod. Mick looked all around and pretended he could not see this huge shaggy haired animal standing not 50 feet away with big horns sticking out of its mangy forehead. "I don't see a thing," he said to Ansel.

"You have to see it. It is standing right over there," Ansel pleaded as he pointed in the general direction.

Mick looked all around and said, "What color is it? Pink? Green? What? I don't see a thing. What does it look like?"

By this time Ansel was a nervous wreck. He grabbed Mickey's arm, leaned against him and pointed right at the big shaggy beast. "It's right there," he said. "I know it is. You have to be able to see it or I am going crazy."

Finally Mickey relented and agreed that yes there were several of them in that pen and told Ansel he had just been teasing him.

At which point Ansel grabbed his old dusty John Deere billed cap from his head and started beating Mickey on the arm and shoulders, making the dust fly. Mick was laughing wildly by this time and trying to evade Ansel's attack with the cap. I'm sure by that time it was too late for Ansel to have to go behind the barn to do his job.

"Whew, dang you Mick" Ansel finally replied. "I thought I was either seeing things or going crazy."

A small family of hippies had also moved near us and we became acquainted with them. I won't tell their name because I'm going to tell a yarn about these guys. They were going to raise a garden so they borrowed all the tools they would need from Mickey.

Their garden had been growing for at least a month and a half when we visited them one day to retrieve our now broken and useless tools. I noticed their radishes were doing quite well and asked them why they weren't picking them.

"Oh," the lady hippie told me, "They aren't ready yet."

Old gardener that I was I found that hard to believe and walked over and started pulling them from the ground. They were amazed to see the bright red radishes coming out of the ground.

"We thought they would grow on top of the leaves like they do in the grocery stores," she told me. This couple did not remain hippies long and took up honest endeavors.

Another time the boys had gotten home from school before I got off work. They called me to say that Ansel was inside our garage. He had been at the front door wanting to come inside and the boys, believing it was OK, admitted him. They were smart enough to know that when he started making suggestive remarks to remove him from the house. They locked the doors and called me at work.

I immediately drove home in high dudgeon and tried to run him off, but he would not budge. He was determined to stay inside our garage and had locked the door and would not let me in.

Angry as a mother bear with cubs I went inside our house and called and talked to the sheriff who knew us and the situation very well.

He asked me how soon Mickey would be home and I told him another hour and a half. He advised me to wait for Mick and allow him to handle the situation. I said that was not good enough he should come down and remove him or I was going to shoot him myself. Boy, I was mad.

The sheriff told me, "Shoot him. It will save the county money." Barring that I should just leave Ansel in the garage and wait for Mickey. That is what I did, but let me tell you I was tempted to shoot him. I could not believe the sheriff himself would tell someone to shoot and kill another person, but that is how life was in Brown County. He knew me well enough to know I would not shoot the old coot.

One year it was extremely cold and Ansel had not succeeded in getting a bed at the state's expense. His little camper trailer had been removed for unknown reasons and he had nowhere to go. He slept anywhere he could find shelter, in abandoned barns or hollow logs, sometimes on hillsides covered only with leaves for protection, he told us. He ate whatever food he was offered or found. Once, wanting alcohol and not having any, he came inside my house and drank every bottle of vanilla and other flavorings I had in the pantry and drank straight rubbing alcohol from the bottle.

Mickey told me about Ansel's plight and asked if he could bring him inside our new home. We had a bed set up in the basement and I agreed he could sleep down there until it warmed up a little. It was warm and not fancy but it beat sleeping inside a cold, drafty barn or on a ravine covered with leaves. He ate from our table but he didn't stay too long because I insisted he take a bath using plenty of warm water and soap before he moved in and then on a fairly regular basis after that. He could endure hunger and cold, sleeping in drafty barns or on hillsides, the hardships of World War II, but he could not abide the thought of bathing regularly and keeping clean.

"Bathing makes me smell like a sissy," he complained.

I told him that if he expected to stay in our house, sleep in our beds and eat at our table I preferred him to smell like a sissy and not a billy goat. He finally relented but made plans to move out as quickly as possible.

While he was soaking in a bathtub full of hot soapy water with a little bleach added for good measure I would hold my nose and gingerly lift his old dirty overalls by one strap with my fingertips and drop them and every stitch he had worn into the washer and wash them. Ansel had to stay in that bathtub and soak until the clothes were both washed and dried because the clothes he had on his back were all he brought with him.

Making him bathe at least once a week got rid of him about as fast as letting him hear me load that shotgun had done.

Back when we first knew Ansel, Mickey and I enjoyed going to the movies. One evening we found a babysitter for the boys and decided to go and see the movie "Who's Afraid of Virginia Wolff." This movie won numerous awards and was considered a classic but neither of us knew the actual plot lines before we left home that night to see it or we never would have gone.

Ansel had gotten into the habit of piling into our car every time we got ready to go somewhere. He never asked if he could go, he just piled in the back seat when he saw us headed toward the car. We had to literally pull or push him from the car so we could go anywhere without him tagging along.

This night we had forcibly removed him from the car and drove up the road about a mile to throw him off the scent of where we were going. Once we were a mile or so up the road we turned around and drove back by our house which was the direction we had wanted to go in the first place.

For some reason I was behind the wheel that night. I have some visual problems and Mickey won't usually ride with me, but that evening I was driving. As we came around a curve in the road Mickey suddenly grabbed the steering wheel from my hands and steered the car sharply to the left. Asking him what in the world he was doing he told me I had nearly run over Ansel.

"Did I miss him," I asked.

"Yes, but you would have run over him if I hadn't grabbed the wheel," Mick said.

"Then let me go back and try it again," I remember telling him.

Ansel had a habit of stashing a spare bottle of wine in the oddest places. Remembering after we left that he had a friend hidden in a nearby culvert he had lain down in the ditch with just his head on the roadway so he could reach into the culvert and retrieve his bottle.

Dressed as he was in the gray sweatshirt and faded blue bibbed overalls and with just his white head on the roadway, in the evening's twilight, I just could not see him. Without Mick's quick action in steering me away from his head I would have driven completely over him.

When we finally made it to the theater after all this drama, trauma and excitement I was so disappointed in the movie I could have cried. For those of you who are not familiar with "Who's Afraid of Virginia Wolff," it is a movie with four drunk people. There is not a sober moment in the entire film.

Here I was, ready for a time out. We had been lucky enough and had money enough to hire a babysitter and pay for tickets to the show. I had ejected one drunk I knew in exchange for four drunks I did not know. What a waste of admission fees that movie was. I don't think I have ever enjoyed attending movies since then. It just ruined me forever I guess.

As badly as I felt about Ansel it worried me a lot as he aged that he had nowhere permanent to live. His family had pretty much given up on him a long time ago and sort of depended on us to help watch over him. When he turned 65 and became eligible for Social Security I started calling area nursing homes and old soldier's homes trying to find a place for him to live.

A nursing home located about 15 miles north of Nashville in Morgantown agreed to take him in and care for him. I notified Ansel's sister and niece and they agreed for him to go to the home and be cared for there.

It was the best thing to happen to Ansel in his adult life. Even though the nursing home was separated from a tavern only by an alley, he never drank again. He liked to go over to the tavern and listen to the music when it was playing, but he always just sipped a soft drink. We never saw him drunk again.

The nursing home kept him clean, well fed, sober and healthy.

Mickey would occasionally go pick Ansel up from the nursing home and take him along with him to visit some customer or to just get him out awhile. Ansel enjoyed Mick's visits but always refused a beer if Mickey offered to stop at The Pine Room Tavern or somewhere and buy him one. But Mick never offered to buy him a beer or bottle of wine once he realized that Ansel really had stopped drinking.

What a difference!! Having a regular income and someone to shelter and care for him allowed Ansel to live the last few years of his life in relative comfort and ease.

General Douglas MacArthur once gave a famous speech and said "Old soldiers never die, they just fade away." That is what Ansel did, he just faded away.

Thanks, Old Soldier.

Susie Ayers

Susie was the widow of Bernell Ayers, and was my husband's aunt. She lived about a quarter of a mile north of where we built our first home in Copperhead Hollow, which is now known as Susie Ayers Road. We bought a two acre lot from her in 1963 for $200 and we were so poor we had to pay the debt off in $10 payments as we got that much put aside. It took us over a year or so to pay her off completely and that little plot was finally all ours. Her house and ours were the first ones built on that road. Later she would sell house sites to others or give them to her children and several other homes would be built but we had moved away before most of that happened.

Susie Ayers, a year or so before she died.

While we were struggling to pay her in full for the lot, she allowed us to go on the property and begin clearing the underbrush and briars. Mickey worked at that chore every spare moment he had.

Once that bill was paid and the clearing completed, we saved up every penny we could generate. When we had at least $50 in our pockets, we would drive our old pickup to a lumberyard and buy $50 worth of building material for the house we would one day build.

Coming up with an extra $50 was extremely difficult for us. Times were hard, jobs did not pay much and children and medical expenses took what little we had. So those $50 amounts took a long time to save.

Usually it would take us most of the day to make a trip for lumber. At that time we sometimes drove all the way to Wick's Lumber in Bloomfield or McCormick's Lumber in Amity. Once there we were allowed to sort the material, and we did, so we could buy only the best.

If the kids got hungry, and I never remember a trip when they didn't, we would stop and buy a pound of bologna, loaf of bread, corn chips, bean dip and pop then stop along the road and have a picnic.

The old truck we had would be nearly dragging on the highway at the rear it would be so heavily laden. That lumber would bounce up and down, the babies would sometimes cry, I might have a headache and Mick was at the end of his rope on some of these trips. But, looking back, I think those were some of the best times in our life together.

Upon returning home the lumber would be carefully sorted by size and stacked in our yard and covered with a tarp to protect it from the weather. We did this several times with those $50 increments until we thought we had enough lumber to get a house under roof.

Grandma Lizzie paid Lloyd Kent, a bulldozer owner/operator who lived in Pike's Peak to come and push out a basement for us. That was a love gift I never forgot.

Finally we were able to build our house and asked my brother Glenn to come and help us start it. The first thing he did was grab up an armload of those precious 2x4s that had cost us so dearly, and start sawing them into various sized pieces. Nearly having a stroke Mickey asked what he thought he was doing. Glenn told Mickey he was building us some sawhorses for a platform to work from. Mickey said OK. We still have those two, now rickety, sawhorses today. They are barely standing on each of their four legs, the tops have been nicked by saws until they are almost cut through, but we keep them as souvenirs.

Finally our house was completed and we moved into it. Susie became our next door neighbor and what times we had with her over the next few years!

We bought a water well drilling rig in March 1968 and started our own home-based business and had our first telephone installed. We were on a party line of four with Susie, her sister Sharlot, and another whom I have forgotten, but it might have been Richard and Mary Aspenson sharing the same line. One member of our party was rarely in residence so that would have been the Aspensons, so that one was no problem. But it was Susie who caused the most problems for us.

Early every morning she would start calling her family and friends and she would talk to each of them for literally hours. Every day, one after the other, she would call those on her round robin file, starting with her sisters Sharlot, married to Howard Fleetwood, and Agnes, who was married to Lloyd Hedrick. It was seldom we could use our phone.

We had spent many precious dollars preparing handout literature advertising our business, passing it out everywhere it looked like someone would need a well. Our phone line was so busy our customers could not reach us. In the afternoon after school let out, I could not call the boys to check on them and they couldn't call me at my work place. We would have to ask her permission to use our telephone and she would get ticked off at us for butting in.

Finally, after about a year of haggling with Susie, we gave up the ghost, called the phone company and had them put in a private line for our use even though it cost us a great deal of money to have the private rather than a residential party line.

That was about the only real problem we ever had with her. Susie would prove to be a good neighbor other than the telephone. She offered to be Lonnie's babysitter after school when he wasn't going to Grandma Lizzie's house. For the great sum of $5 per week she did my laundry and ironed it, having it ready for me to pick up when I got home from work. What a godsend that boon was for me.

The woman got out of bed by 4 a.m., threw my clothes in the washer and had them blowing merrily in the wind by daylight. Along about noon, they would be ironed and placed on hangers, the remainder folded into the baskets. I never understood how anyone could rise that early in the morning and start working productively but Susie did it day after day.

She was kind enough to allow us space on her farm to plant a large garden every year and we raised nearly every bite of food we ate. Mickey and the boys and I worked in those gardens every night and morning in the summer. They weeded, hoed and picked. In the evenings after I got home from work and supper was over with, we started canning and freezing. Often it would be 11 p.m. before I crawled into bed. But we were young and it never hurt us a bit to work hard.

In August, 1968, Susie, the boys, and I drove to town one day. On the way home we saw that Mickey was on a job site so we stopped to visit a few minutes. The boys begged to ride home with their dad and I said OK. On the way home Mickey let his helper, Ansel Hillenburg, out of the truck. A half mile further down the road either the truck's door did not latch properly when Ansel got out or it came open accidentally and Doug was thrown from the vehicle onto the roadway, receiving serious injuries. I was far enough behind them that I did not see the accident actually happen for which I am eternally grateful. Seeing my babies bleed like that didn't do me much good.

I left Lonnie with Susie and rode in the ambulance with Doug to the Columbus hospital. Mick followed us in our car. When I got to the hospital Doug did not know me because of his head injury and was blinded, but kept shouting he wanted "his" Lonnie. Even though he could not see anything at that point, (his sight would later return) he knew Lonnie was not nearby. About that time, in through the emergency room doors walked Susie with Lonnie in tow. He had fussed so much worrying about Doug that she did something she rarely did. She drove with him into Columbus herself so Lonnie could see that Doug would live. Once he arrived Doug consented to treatment but Lonnie had to stand by and hold his hand through the whole ordeal. Though unorthodox, I think even the doctors were glad to see Lonnie arrive with Susie.

As Susie began aging she started having some mental disturbance. She wasn't crazy by any means; she was just near to having a nervous breakdown over some past events in her life. It was not unusual for her to call me at 1 or 2 o'clock in the morning, crying hysterically, and asking me to come to her house and sit with her.

Susie Ayers as she appeared while working in a restaurant in Nashville.

Over several weeks I went there many times. She spent the entire time telling me everything that was on her mind and why she was upset. Finally she would be able to sleep and I would slip out of the house and go back to mine and return to my warm bed. During the daylight hours she would have doubts and ask me not to tell what she had told me and I assured her I would never reveal her secrets.   I never have to this day told another soul what she told me. In fact, if you asked me now what she said I could not say. I have completely erased her problems from my memory bank.

I kept telling Susie that I could not help her; that she needed professional help. For a long time she refused then she finally admitted herself to a mental health facility and they were able to work with her and resolved her problems. After that she found a job and for the next few years, even though she was getting on in age, she worked in Nashville making pizzas and she loved her job. Occasionally I would order a take-out pizza for my family's supper and she would pile about double the amount of toppings on my order as a way of thanking me.

I had always wanted to know how to make homemade noodles and I had heard everyone rave about what good ones Susie made. She came to my house one day for a cooking lesson and showed me by making a batch at my own kitchen counter and I learned how she made them. I still make them occasionally and they are delicious.

Aunt Susie's Egg Noodles

Put 3 or 4 cups of all purpose flour in a small, deep bowl and punch a hole with your fist down into the middle. Into that hole

place two whole eggs, two ½ eggshells of milk, ½ tsp. salt, ½ tsp baking powder and 3 drops of yellow food coloring. This is not rocket science so if you want to make a bigger batch, use more flour, eggs and milk as desired, but this amount makes a large number of noodles.

Mix all together with your fingers, drawing the flour into the wet mix as needed until you have a fairly firm, almost dry ball. Open a brown grocery bag to its fullest and place it on a large flat surface and flour generously. Place the ball onto the paper and knead and roll with a rolling pin until it is the thickness you desire.

You may have to add more flour as you roll the noodles to keep them from sticking to the brown bag. If they are too wet, just lift the rolled noodles and sprinkle some more flour below and on top of the batter as needed to keep them movable on the brown paper. When ready, cut to size. You may use a noodle or pizza cutter or simply a knife. I have a hand-held noodle cutter I found in a yard sale a few years ago and it is terrific; every noodle is exactly as wide as its neighbor. If cutting by hand, try to cut each strip to about the same size for more even cooking and appearance.

Ideally you should let the noodles dry about three hours. But, if you are in a big hurry, it doesn't hurt to use them as soon as they are rolled out. When ready to cook, bring beef or chicken broth (bullion may be used) to a boil in a large container. Drop the noodles by small handfuls into the boiling broth, stirring gently after each addition. Add until all the noodles are in the broth then turn to simmer, cover the pan and let them cook until

the noodles are very tender, about 20 minutes. You will need to stir them gently occasionally.

Once all the noodles are cooking cleanup is a breeze. Just fold up the brown paper bag from several directions and place the remaining mess in the garbage.

My sister, Anna, loved my noodles and tried to make her own once using this method. I asked her how they turned out.

"I swear, Helen," she said, "I think we ate half that paper bag."

She evidently had not kept enough flour below her noodles when she was rolling them out. I never have that problem and I don't recall Susie ever telling me about it either.

The other dish Susie made that I never perfected no matter how many times I tried to duplicate her efforts was the simple pork roast. She would just buy a big chunk of fairly inexpensive lean pork and everything turned out delicious. Her roasts were always slightly salty, browned to perfection, and so tender it was amazing. I have tried several times to duplicate this, even going so far as to buy a large chunk of pork tenderloin, but my pork roasts never turned out like hers.

Susie died in 2005 and was buried in Mt. Zion Cemetery. Five children and several grand- and great-grandchildren survive her.

Dave Williamson

Dave and Mickey were best friends from their youngest school days and shared some amazing adventures over their lifetimes. It is a wonder, hearing them tell the tales when they get together, that either of them lived to a ripe old age. Anyone else would have been accidentally killed, shot on purpose or been badly wounded if they tried some of the tricks these two men shared in their youth.

While they were students in Van Buren High School the two boys were constantly in trouble with their principal Ralph Waldo McCullough and a few of the teachers. I met Mr. McCullough for the first time during last year's Van Buren School reunion. He said he didn't remember the guys being "too" bad. Maybe he, like me, has lost some of his memory? I wouldn't think anyone could forget the stunts these students pulled.

For a conservation project one year they built fodder shocks near the school. A fire broke out in one of the shocks one day and all the boys got to run outside and throw water on the blaze. Then another shock burst into flame, and then another. As soon as one shock was extinguished, another would light up. The fun was over when Mr. McCullough saw Dave running behind yet another shock to light it and realized what was happening.

Ralph Waldo McCullough, now 84, in 2006. He was a
very young principal at Van Buren High School.

Another project required the class to build a wildlife project in the
nearby woods. Dave took the whole class into the woods, walking a
long way, explaining his project was just around the next corner, at
least right around here somewhere, he would say. Then he claimed to
be lost. Then the friends with them said yes, they could see the project
and would point up into the general area, but Mr. McCullough said
he could not see it—there probably wasn't one but the friends stuck
together. Finally, two hours later at lunchtime, Dave circled back to
the school with an exhausted but smarter Mr. McCullough in tow.

Dave and Liz Williamson.

Another time Mr. McCullough had a new car, drove it to school and got it hung up in the mud. He asked some of the older boys to help push it out and of course Mickey and Dave and a few others volunteered. The teacher was revving the engine and yelling for the boys to push, push harder! Instead of pushing the boys lifted the rear end of the car off the ground, pulling backwards, allowing the car's tires to spin but without being on the ground. When the teacher got out to see what more needed to be done to free the car, the boys just looked perplexed and said they couldn't push it out. Finally the teacher caught them in the act and amid much laughter they released the car from the mud.

Dave and Mickey once put a horse inside Dave's dad's house. It all started when the Omar bread company delivery man came to the home to deliver bread and rolls, as was the custom back then. There was an Omar and a Bewley Bread Company that both had routes in this area. The Omar delivery man, Raymond Mattox, would give a two-note whistle and sing out "O-mar" to alert the homeowners of his presence. If the homeowner was not at home, he would just open the door and leave their bread order inside.

When he arrived one day the guys were ready for him. Dave and Mickey had placed a full grown horse inside the front door. When the Omar man opened the door to leave his goods, there stood the horse. He threw his goodies inside the house, slammed the door and ran away to his truck.

Mick saw Mr. Mattox many years later in Columbus and got to talking with him. Mr. Mattox remembered the incident with the horse, but did not know that Mickey had been involved. It was stuff like this, usually thought up by Dave that would make his name a legend in history as a practical joker.

Mickey and Dave got along great; Dave and I did not. We fussed constantly after Mickey and I were married. All Dave and I had to do to have an altercation was for me to see him walk into our home and the feuding began. Dave knew this and he pushed my buttons every chance he got.

He had married young, almost as soon as he and Mickey had graduated from high school, and had three children before Mickey even thought of marrying. By the time Mickey and I got married Dave had gone through a messy divorce.

He would come to our house to get Mick to go somewhere with him and when I objected he would tell Mickey to "tell her to go to hell." That would make me so mad I could have taken a ball bat to his head. I say today that he wanted Mickey to be as miserable as he was.

Finally Dave remarried and our ability to get along picked up a bit.

Our boys called him "Crazy Dave" because they had heard and seen so much about him as they were growing up.

Dave would do things to annoy other people. Once he drove his old Jeep through a big discarded pile of farm fencing on a nearby farm, scattering it down the road for a mile. Because the neighbors had seen the Jeep parked at our house they assumed it was ours and blamed Mickey when in reality it was Dave's doings. Dave just left his Jeep parked at our place in case we needed or wanted to use it. Mickey ended up cleaning up the fence mess along the road because Dave would not own up to the deed.

Another thing Dave did on a frequent basis was try to cross a creek or climb a hill with his automobile, knowing the vehicle was not set up to do this. He just wanted to see if it would go where he wanted it to go. Usually he got hung up in the creek or slid off the hillside and had to be rescued and you know who got to ride to the rescue, Mickey. These kinds of stunts usually occurred during the night time hours and it was usual for Dave to show up at our house about 2 a.m. asking to be rescued.

His Dad, Burr Williamson and his mom, Goldie (another sister of Aunt Susie), would just shake their heads at his shenanigans. They were as much at a loss about him as I and others always seemed to be.

Our two boys loved to watch Saturday morning cartoons as they were growing up. Nearly every Saturday for a long time Crazy Dave would drop by to have a cup of coffee with Mickey and watch cartoons with the boys. He would yell at Wiley E. Coyote to, "stop being stupid" as he chased the roadrunner. "You have fallen off that same damn mountain a thousand times," he would shout. It was amusing to the boys and they had so much fun laughing at him that that is why they dubbed him Crazy Dave.

At one time Dave got a little tipsy. One morning about 3 a.m. he came to our house, blowing the car's horn for the entire length of the driveway, rousing our whole house. I crawled out of my warm bed, admitted him and saw that he was drunker than ten skunks and ran him off. He wanted me to get out of bed and fix him some breakfast.

I told him to go home and let his wife fix him some breakfast but he advised me she wouldn't get out of bed and do it. After about the third or fourth time of him returning to our house that night I was ready to string him up. Finally after hours of making a nuisance of himself he went home and went to bed. This was typical Dave behavior.

One other thing our boys always thought was funny about Dave was his obsessive neatness with his hand tools. His small garage had every hand tool known to man hanging on the wall. That would have been all right to have them at hand, but Dave stored his a little differently than most. Each time he bought a hand tool he would place it against the white of his pegboard and draw a black outline of the tool. From that time on, that tool had to be in that outlined place at all times. But even with all these tools available to him, I don't recall him ever fixing or repairing things very often. Usually if he needed some kind of mechanical work done he would call for Mickey's assistance. It nearly drove Mick crazy when he would lay a tool down temporarily while fixing something for Dave and Dave would immediately grab it and place it back where its silhouette was drawn on the pegboard.

His widow, Liz, told me last week that when he reached his mid-fifties, he quit being this obsessive and mellowed out. That had to have been like having a different man living in your house.

Dave was also just as obsessive about his garden. Not a weed was allowed to grow in it the entire summer. Every plant had to be set apart from its neighbor just so with no weeds in between. Long after everyone else had "laid by" their garden, meaning they no longer had to cultivate and weed it, Dave kept his rows pristine clean.

A really strange thing happened this morning as Mickey and I drove to Maxine Fleetwood's home to pick up her pictures for this book. We were speaking of Dave as we drove along, wondering how he was doing in his second fight against cancer. When we arrived at Maxine's the first thing she told us was that he had died today, March 23, 2006.

His name is brought up in this book to show some of the quirky, sometimes funny neighbors and relationships we have had in the Story community over the years.

Dave was 68 years old when he died of cancer last week. His wife, Elizabeth (Liz) Baron Williamson survives along with his four children, Kim, Dawn, Darren and Nancy; seven grandchildren; five great-grandchildren; and brothers Rod and Ron. Per Dave's wishes his body was cremated and no funeral was held.

Orville and Olivia Toler

Orville and Olivia, notice how both names start with the letter O and sound somewhat similar and how frequently things like this happen, lived on down State Road 135 South from Story near Houston Road. Their home is the lovely place known as Cherry Hill; a long, white old-timey home with long porches and a colorful past.

A picture of the Toler home shows the glassed in porch on the right end where a former resident, Harriet Widmer served pancake breakfasts to visitors.

I learned while writing this book that Buck and Harriet Widmer were former residents of Cherry Hill. For many years, Mrs. Widmer played the Aunt Jemima Syrup character on radio commercials. She also was the voice of Miss Blue on the old Amos and Andy radio show. Although she was not a Negro, Mrs. Widmer was a talented enough actress to make her role convincing, Al Donaldson said.

While she lived at Cherry Hill, she would prepare and serve pancake breakfasts to visitors on one of her back porches. "I'm sure she used Aunt Jemima syrup," Olivia said.

Both the Tolers are hot Republicans and work hard for their party's candidates. Olivia worked as a real estate broker here in Brown County for many years. In fact, she is the one who sold us the farm where we presently reside. Orville was a manufacturer's representative and a flyer of small airplanes in his spare time. That is one of the major ways we got acquainted with the Tolers.

The Tolers: Olivia, Tamsin, Bill and Orville. Their Siamese cat, Miss Blue (named after Miss Blue on the Amos and Andy radio show) is in Olivia's arms. A former owner of their farm, Harriet Widmer was the voice of Miss Blue on that radio program.

For our son Lonnie's ninth birthday celebration, Mickey and I took him and Douglas to Walesboro Airport near Columbus where we rented a small plane and pilot. The pilot flew us all over the southern half of Brown County. The hills were beautiful, wearing their fall coat of many colors that late October day. This little trip sparked an interest for flying in Lonnie that would be stoked on a regular basis by Orville Toler and another of our friends, Bob Bohall.

Orville was the owner of a fairly rare, highly desirable type of collectible airplane called a Luscombe. He was proud of the plane and built his own runway on his farm so it could be parked in a garage/hangar on his own place when not in use. Formerly, he had had to keep it at Freeman Field in Seymour which was about 30 miles away.

Orville's little Luscombe airplane. A neighbor took this picture from his own plane while both were flying. Orville has sold the little plane and bought a different one since this picture was taken.

By having his own runway, when he wanted to take an afternoon spin, he just rolled the little Luscombe out and flew off into the horizon for an hour or so. We live about a mile as the crow flies from

Orville and we often watched him flying around. Finally one day Lonnie asked him to let him go up with him.

Now both Orville and Lonnie were pretty good size guys by this time and it was just about all the little Luscombe wanted to do to get off the ground. They said they had to use every inch of runway Orville had to get it into the air. From that time on, Lonnie was fired up on flying and Orville fed the flames. He encouraged Lonnie to pursue his dream, even occasionally allowing him to ride to the Seymour airport with him.

For a couple of years Lonnie worked at odd jobs for his dad and saved every penny he could not be tempted to spend on something else, and kept that money for his flying lessons. In 1977 he and Douglas operated our well drilling business the entire summer while their dad worked as a deputy sheriff. He saved every penny he earned for pilot lessons. When he was 15, still too young to drive on the roadways, he began taking private flying lessons at Freeman Field in Seymour.

I would load my laundry up in the car, take both boys with me, and drop Lonnie at the airport for his lessons. Since I could not stand to watch him going up, coming down, losing altitude and all the other things he had to learn, I would find the area laundromat and wash our clothes. By the time I was finished with that chore Doug would have his homework completed and Lonnie would be down on terra firma again. I could breathe a sigh of relief.

One Sunday afternoon I was sitting alone at the airport while Lonnie was soloing. Orville came in to visit with the manager. The manager told Orville he needed to test fly an airplane for a customer and asked the two of us if we wanted to fly with him. He was only going as far as Louisville, KY. So we each said yes and got into the plane.

We were flying along at 180 MPH when the pilot asked me what kind of turn I wanted to make. Well, I didn't have a clue, so I told him anything he wanted to do was fine by me. That pilot took me at my word and immediately made a turn, going upside down in a partial loop in the process and still at that speed.

At that speed, Orville and I were both nearly strangled as we dangled upside down in our seatbelts. We were both furious with that pilot and never flew with him again.

The Tolers are now retired. They spend their winters on their sailboat or in a little cabin in Florida or sailing around in the Caribbean. You can count on them to return to Brown County every spring, especially if there is an election to be conducted or if the morel mushrooms are in season.

They now have new neighbors building a home/hangar on a part of their property. The young man is also a fan of flying and owns a couple of planes and will share runway space with Orville.

The Tolers have two children, Bill and Tamsin, known locally as Elizabeth, and three grandchildren. Tamsin decided when she was 18 and others started calling her Liz, to begin using her middle name as her legal name.

It must be an election year because I called their number last week and they had just returned to Van Buren the evening before, and no, they had not had time yet to go mushroom hunting, but they will as soon as they can get unpacked, Olivia assured me.

*This isVan Buren artist Kenneth Reeve at work. Noted photographer
and artist/neighbor of Mr. Reeve, George Bredewater, caught him at
work one day and took this photograph. It may have been the day
he was working on the etching of the Toler property shown below.*

*This is an ink etching of the Toler's home by artist Kenneth Reeve
who lived for many years just down the road a piece from the
Tolers. Ken and his wife, Helen, moved to the East coast last year.*

Kenneth and Jewel Carmichael

Kenneth and Jewel lived on State Road 135 East from Story between Bob Hedrick's place and Mickey's Granny Ayers' home. Jewel was a homemaker and a beautiful woman, active in 4-H and working with children of the county. They were the parents of our one-time landlady, Sheila Lucas and her sister, Phyllis Lucas. The two sisters married brothers, Jack and Ed Lucas from Elkinsville. Kenneth was the principal for many years at the Van Buren Elementary School at Stone Head.

Kenneth Carmichael when he was principal
at Van Buren Elementary School.

Kenneth had to have gotten a belly full of me while my kids were students at his school but he never acted like he minded me being in his office so frequently. It seems like I was at the school at least once a week raising cane about something or other.

When Lonnie started elementary school the PTO organization was barely operating. There were only about six or eight people who attended the meetings and the president of the organization would open every meeting by saying "I'm sorry, I'm just not prepared tonight." I would get so mad. I really wanted to become involved but there was nothing to get involved with. When it came time for the annual election of officers someone placed my name in the hat for president and I was elected.

I was determined to not only be prepared for each meeting but to make a difference during my tenure as president. Although it meant a lot of work for me—I had a full time job at the time—I had a program prepared for every monthly meeting. For some programs we might show a video, have a special speaker or hold a carnival. But every meeting saw something really special presented.

The membership grew from the original six or eight people to a gymnasium overflowing with participants interested in Van Buren Elementary School and its activities. One night I showed a farm safety video that had been loaned to me by the Columbus Library.

Farmer, conservation officer and later Brown County Sheriff, Rex Kritzer came up to me after the meeting and put his artificial arm around my shoulder. He asked if the movie had been directed toward him. He had lost his right arm to a corn picker a few years prior to this; having to cut the remaining threads of his arm off with his knife himself to save his life. To keep himself from bleeding to death after cutting his arm off, he used his belt to fashion a tourniquet, he told me.

Wearing an artificial arm with a hook prosthesis he was but one of the many farm people in this community to be injured by farm machinery. I mentioned in another chapter that Lloyd, Ralph, Bob and Ted Hedrick had been killed or injured severely in farm accidents so the movie I showed applied to all farmers in that area.

While I was the PTO president one of my goals was to erect a chain link fence in front of the school's playground to prevent the children from running out onto the state highway to chase a ball. At that time there was a bridge on the highway at either end of the playground that had a curve at each end of the bridges. Once a vehicle came out of either of these bridges they would speed up as they went by the school. Many times I had seen children chasing loose balls across the road. I wanted to stop that so I asked Kenneth if it was OK if the PTO paid for and erected the fence.

He told me, "Helen, we have never had a child get hurt out there. I don't know if we need a fence or not."

I asked him to reconsider, "Kenneth, how many children getting hurt would it take to change your mind and think it was enough?" Without another word he assented to having the fence erected. Its purpose was not to hem the kids in exactly, but to stop their forward motion into the roadway. If they had to stop and think before climbing over the fence, or running around to the end of it to get to the roadway, it would take them a few extra seconds and maybe save their life, I reasoned.

Later the state highway would replace and straighten those two bridges, making it a straight shot by the school. It would turn out that the fence was needed after all. Not too many years after the road was straightened, a car went through the fence, knocking a lot of it down. Had the accident occurred during daylight hours, several children playing on the ball fields could have been hurt if not killed. After many years of use and/or repair, it was recently replaced and made longer and continues to serve its purpose.

Kenneth learned early on that I would be taking an active part in my children's education. I could remember my own sadistic second and fifth grade teachers and was determined that none of my kid's teachers would ever take advantage of my kids, so I was at the school early and often.

During Lonnie's third grade he had a teacher who was absolutely insane. She picked at him constantly for every infraction, one being that he "ran" in the hallways. It was her habit when her class was going in or out of the classroom to walk in a line. She would tell me Lonnie was "running" when in actuality he was just taking normal steps for a boy his size with such long legs.

Lonnie was always very tall as a child and his normal steps would be about double those of some others in his class, giving the impression he was running, when he really wasn't.

I once received a note on his report card from this teacher that I could not decipher no matter how hard I tried or which way I turned it. It was totally illegible. I took the card with me to school the next morning and asked Kenneth to look at it. He couldn't figure her message out either so when the teacher entered the building he called her to the office and asked what her note said. She told us that she was reporting to me that she "could not read Lonnie's handwriting!"

Kenneth and I went with her to the classroom to talk with Lonnie and ask him what his problem was. There he sat with his desk sitting on top of his lap trying to do his school work. Every time he tried to write or draw lines the desk would wobble from one side to the other on his knees. She was so silly that she had not attempted to find a larger desk from an upper classroom for him to use, forcing him to use a desk a small child would need. When Kenneth saw what the problem was he immediately went and got a desk from the sixth grade classroom and brought it in for Lonnie to use and thus solved that problem. She was punishing Lonnie for being tall.

Lonnie was a nervous wreck this whole school year with this teacher screaming and yelling at him on a daily basis. Kenneth told me she arrived at school each morning, crying as though her heart would break. Something was terribly wrong with this woman, he said.

Kenneth and Jewel Carmichael on their 35th wedding anniversary.

As the school year was winding down Kenneth asked me to stop by and talk with him. He knew that the current fourth grade teacher also talked loudly and said that that might not be best for Lonnie. He said he had asked this teacher to teach the third grade the following year and allow him to hire a different fourth grade teacher so Lonnie would not have to go through another year of yelling. The teacher he replaced was a very nice woman, she just talked loudly, but it worked for Lonnie and I have always thanked Kenneth and her for letting him have a quiet teacher.

Kenneth's replacement of the fourth grade teacher would be a Godsend for us. That was the year that Mickey had to have his heart surgery. Lonnie began that school year not knowing whether his beloved dad would be alive or not, but thankfully, everything went fine with the experimental surgery.

Then Douglas started school and more problems arose. He was always getting a head injury, most of the time while on school property. He had a teacher, I think she was just his playground supervisor, who injured him badly. One day she had the classes lined up to return inside the school building, which they were supposed to enter in a quiet manner so as not to disturb the classes not then at recess.

I was told by some students that Douglas kept talking to his friends and she decided to take action. She grabbed Douglas in front on both sides of his head, shaking his head backward and forwards as she emphasized her orders to be quiet. Perhaps not realizing what she was doing, she was hitting his head against the brick wall of the school building each time she pushed his head backwards. He immediately became ill and was sent to the "sick room" where he remained until time for the buses to take the kids home.

When I got home that night I looked at the back of his head and it was scraped raw where it had hit the building so many times. Several of the kids in Doug's class called me asking about him. Since he had been taken to the sick room immediately after the altercation, they had not seen or talked with him since the incident and were concerned because they knew to watch out for him to help him avoid head injuries. Each one of them told me the same story about this teacher shaking Douglas and hitting his head against the wall. I was furious.

The next morning I drove to the school with Douglas in tow and we went straight to Kenneth's office. I explained the situation and showed him the back side of Doug's head. Kenneth was appalled to see what this teacher had done to Doug. By that time the entire back of his head was streaked with scabs and he still had a horrible headache.

When Kenneth called the teacher into his office as she entered the building, I was ready, fighting mad and immediately started yelling at her. She, of course, denied harming Douglas in any way. Turning Douglas around, I showed her the scraping across the back of his head and explained how many brain concussions he had had and told her she could have killed him. I explained how many kids had called asking about Doug the previous evening and told Kenneth and the teacher what the kids had had to say. She still denied she had done anything to harm him.

At that point I got into her face as Kenneth sat there speechless and I told her if she ever touched my kid again I would kill her. She could tell I meant exactly what I said. I believe Kenneth did also, but he made no move to shush me. Finally he dismissed her; she was later fired as had been the third grade teacher that Lonnie had had to put up with.

Douglas was a very smart young boy and as his head kept getting hurt more and more often, the other kids in his class looked out for him. They also expected him to excel at anything he attempted. He loved making things for the science fairs held each year. Kenneth Carmichael encouraged each child to enter the fairs each year.

One year Doug's project was a xylophone made by suspending glass pop bottles partially filled with water from a bar he had made. Each pop bottle represented another note on the musical scale. For the striker, he used a hammer he had made from his Tinker Toys, and wrote out a couple of simple songs that could be played on the bottles. He had carefully measured how much water was needed in each bottle to make the proper note sound.

His project took second place to another young boy's project that had been made almost entirely by the other boy's dad. The project was too sophisticated for a young boy to have made by himself.

The kids knew the other boy's parent had made his and that Doug had designed and made his own project. In protest of Doug's project earning second instead of first place, these young kids held a sit-in demonstration. But the judges of the event would not change their minds. I thought this was so cute of these kids to stick up for Douglas in this manner and it goes a long way to show the esteem they had for him. It also reinforced my belief in the phone calls I had received from them the day the teacher had injured his head. I knew they had told me the truth, and the teacher had lied. I think Kenneth realized she had lied also.

I have always been grateful to Kenneth for the way he protected and stood up for my kids. He did not have to do that, and he probably could have had me arrested for threatening to kill one of his teachers, but instead he upheld my kids. He knew them both very well and he knew they were very smart, well-behaved kids who meant no disrespect to anyone.

Kenneth has been dead for many years now and my kids are middle-aged men. Jewel, 91, still resides in her home on State Road 135 near Story. She and her daughter Phyllis occasionally assist her grandson, JD Lucas with his nursery business which was aptly named "Gram's Nursery," for her own love of beautiful flowers.

Douglas Ayers, in foreground, sets off a model rocket he made for a science fair as the other students look on.

This is the still youthful looking Jewel Carmichael, now 91, helping her grandson in his Gram's Nursery business which was named for her because of her love of beautiful flowers.

Louis and Mabel Henderson

My introduction to the Henderson couple was traumatic to say the least. Mickey and I had moved to the Stone Head community in 1962 from Bartholomew County where we had lived for a year or so. We had moved from our first house in Story in early October 1960 to Bartholomew County but we got homesick for Brown County and decided to return. We moved to Stone Head when Lonnie was about a year old.

It was there in Harold and Velma Seitz's log home rental at Stone Head that we would live when Douglas was born in March 1963. At that time I stayed home with the kids for a time because Doug was nursing and I wanted to spend some time with both of the boys.

Two or three times a week I would take the kids for a walk, usually to Eleanor Clark's grocery store in Pikes Peak. That was a fair walk, about a mile and a half each way, but I enjoyed walking at that time and it gave the boys some fresh air. Mickey finally bought me a little red wagon to use on our walks and that made it easier for me to handle two little boys.

A George Bredewater drawing of the front
of the Pike's Peak General Store.

As we came to the intersection at Stone Head the house directly in front of us was the Hendricks's house. I believe his name was John, but I cannot recall his wife's name. The thing I remember about her was she made the best dill pickles I ever tasted. Every time she saw us coming she would go to a big stone crock and have a dill pickle ready for Lonnie when we got there. He loved them with a passion and still does.

They, like most other older couples, loved kids but didn't get to see enough of them. So when they saw us walking they always invited me to stop for a few minutes for a visit and a pickle. They oohed and aahed over the baby Douglas and listened to Lonnie jabber. After that, we would then continue our walk to Pike's Peak.

It was on one of these walks that I would meet Mabel Henderson at Eleanor's store.

Louis and Mabel Henderson, in their twilight years.

When the boys and I got to her store I might need an item or two. Whatever I might need couldn't amount to much because I also had to carry Douglas back home with whatever I had bought until I got the little red wagon. I would walk around inside the store with the baby in my arms and Lonnie tugging at my britches leg. I was a really careful Mom because I had no experience with child rearing except what I was learning from these two boys. They were my guinea pigs.

As I was going around the store, Doug in a blanket in my arms, this older woman just took him out of my arms and started cooing to him and looking right down into his face, pushing his blanket back with the dirtiest hands I had every seen on a grown woman.

Who was this woman I wondered. There she stood with green rubber boots on, covered with who knew what from the barnyard, with a coat just as covered with dirt and she had grabbed my baby!

Lonnie had by then made up with Eleanor who he knew would give him a banana before he left her store if he smiled sweetly to her. This became such a habit that when I would be shopping with him in other stores, he would reach out of the grocery cart and grab a banana and start eating it. When we got to the checkout counter I would have to have them weigh a banana that was about the size of the one he ate so I could pay for it. I finally had to make Eleanor stop giving them to him to keep both of us out of trouble in other stores.

Eleanor Clark in her grocery story in Pike's Peak.

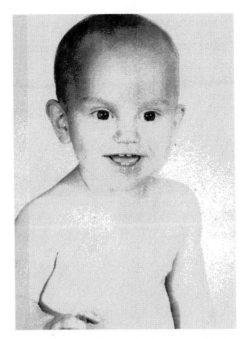

Lonnie was the baby banana thief.

I did not know Mabel from Adam but she knew exactly who I was. She had known Mickey his whole life but I had never met her. Eleanor introduced us when she saw my anxiety and I took my baby back from Mabel's dirty arms.

I was so scared he would "catch" something from this woman I was worried sick. But he was OK and when I returned home and told Mickey my story about meeting her, he got hysterical laughing. He would never let me forget my first reaction to Mabel.

"She is one of the best women I have ever known," he explained. "A little dirt won't hurt those boys." Apparently it didn't hurt them because they remained hale and hearty much to my relief. And in future years they would get just as dirty when we became well drillers.

Mabel and Louis owned a farm a half mile or so west of Stone Head, across the road from Rex Kritzer but slightly more west than his place and they were childless. They would turn out to be great and loyal friends of ours over the next few years.

Louis and Mabel were an extremely close couple. Wherever you saw one of them you would see both. If Louis was driving the tractor, Mabel would be standing on the drawbar holding on to him with her arms around his waist. If he was in the hayfield, then that is where you would find her. They were never apart.

They would buy a new car about once every 15 years and drive it, usually at 10 miles an hour or so, until there was not a scrap of it left holding together. For the last two or three thousand miles they drove their cars, the fenders and bumpers would be literally flapping in the wind they were so worn through and damaged by rust and dents. When their cars reached that condition, only then would they buy another. That car might haul the two of them, or hay, hogs, or whatever else needed hauling on the farm.

A car was not just a mode of transportation to them, it was a farm tool. Everyone made fun of their automobiles which were usually a large Buick model or something like that in size. When they got done with one and had decided it would not make it another mile they would call Clinton Cooley, a junkyard dealer at Gnaw Bone, and tell him to come and get the old one. By that time there wasn't much for him to haul away.

In later years, Mabel had circulation problems in her legs. She lost first one leg and then the other, bits at a time, so she had to have several amputations and became at first wheelchair-ridden and then finally bed-ridden. Louis would sit there by her side for hours at a time, holding her hand, looking out the picture window, asking her to eat something or just reminiscing with her. It was so incredibly sweet watching this couple together.

Louis installed a wheelchair lift along his basement stairs so Mabel could be lifted upstairs to the kitchen. In even later years, after Mabel was dead, the lift could be used by him. By that time he had become almost helpless with crippling arthritis.

Louis enjoyed entertaining me with his fiddle prowess. He, Doc and Hep Beauchamp, Wilma Spiker and other friends started the Bean Blossom Jamboree many years prior to this picture being taken.

When Mabel died Louis asked a relative to live in the upstairs half of his house to help take care of him. In the last years of his life good friends would do that for him. For the most part he lived in the basement apartment with his little dog after Mabel was gone.

Each Thanksgiving I would visit him and take him a dinner the EMTs had prepared. I never accepted money from him, the dinner was given freely; but Louis was determined to "pay" me something for the meal. An emergency medical friend and I started cooking this free Thanksgiving Dinner several years ago, probably around 1982 and the tradition still is going today.

Each fall when he knew the cane was being harvested and sorghum was being boiled down, he sent someone up around Trafalgar to buy him several quarts of sorghum to last him throughout the winter and until the next harvest time.

When I took the Thanksgiving dinner to him, I had to accept one of the jars of sorghum. That was my "pay" for providing him his Thanksgiving dinner and visiting with him a few minutes.

Even though the housekeepers would be cooking a huge Thanksgiving dinner on the floor above where he lived, he refused their offer of a meal, they told me.

"He's downstairs just waiting for you," they would say.

As I look back I think how sad it was that he had to wait from one Thanksgiving to another to visit with me. Sometimes I wish I had visited more often, but when you are young you get busy raising your family and you don't think about things like this until it is too late.

Rest in peace, Louis and Mabel, together again at last.

Anyone knowing the families I have mentioned in this book will recognize George Bredewater's drawing of Hep Beauchamp (L) Louis Henderson, and Wilma Spiker (R). They along with Doc Beauchamp were responsible for starting what is now the Bill Monroe Bluegrass Festival in Bean Blossom.

Paul Lucas & Family

Paul Lucas was truly a law unto himself. He was the father of a good friend of ours who lived for a time with Mickey's Grandma Lizzie. Paul's son, Noah Lee Roy, (we always just call him Lee Roy) would remain friends with us throughout our lives.

Paul is now dead as is his wife, Violet. She died of cancer when Lee Roy was quite young, he told me. There were also two daughters in this family, Barbara and Sharon.

Mickey and I had been married for several years before I met Barbara and Sharon. All of us had congregated that particular day at Paul's home on Whitehorse Road northeast of Bellsville. He was remarried by that time to a woman named Leonie and they called us to come and see them since all three of Paul's children were there visiting that day.

I was sitting in the kitchen feeling kind of left out of things because I did not know all those people when I felt someone standing behind me running their fingers through my hair. I have naturally curly hair and I guess she could not believe it and she was running her fingers through the curls and watching them spring back. That was my introduction to Lee Roy's sister Barbara Seitz (Mrs. Max) and she turned out to be very nice.

When I first met Paul he had already moved away from Elkinsville. His property was purchased by the Army Corps of Engineers to make way for the floodwaters of the Monroe Reservoir.

Paul and Violet Lucas, 1934, on their wedding day.

I believe it was about 1976 or thereabouts when I got better acquainted with Paul. I had been aware of him, but not well acquainted with him prior to that time. In 1976, in celebration of our nation's birthday, I threw my hat into the political ring for county commissioner on the Democratic ticket. I was no politician but I was willing to learn. As soon as Paul heard I was running for a county-wide office, he came to the house to have a little talk with me. He wanted to offer me his best advice on how to get elected.

Once I heard what had gone on in elections of the distant past I was stunned. The stories Paul told me were unbelievable, but undoubtedly true. I had previously heard many similar stories prior to hearing his about how elections were run in "the good old days." He told me how votes were sometimes bought with a bottle of whiskey, a ride to the polls or a bit of money.

Party members would pick a voter up and drive them to the polls to vote. He admitted, they might even have taken the voter to several precincts to cast a ballot; and that sometimes they actually succeeded.

Times were different back then and because of the isolationism in Van Buren Township not everyone knew everyone else. After the road system was improved nearly everyone knew everyone else since there wasn't much population change in the county. Today it is different again because there are so many newcomers to the county. Transportation between towns in earlier times was a big event so few took the long rides or walks. Usually, the people stayed pretty close to home, so this made it possible for Paul and others to convince poll workers in other precincts that this man, who maybe no one at the polls actually knew personally, really resided in their precinct and should be allowed to vote. Most of the poll workers would have known Paul probably because he went around to other places frequently and they would have trusted him to be telling them the truth. Things have tightened up considerably since these long ago days. Beginning this year you have to show a photo identification card in order to cast a ballot.

First, though, in order to get a ride to the polls the voter had to agree to vote for the party's man. In return, the voter would receive a jug of whiskey or a sum of money. If Paul later found out the voter had lied to him and instead had voted for the opposition, that voter would be in trouble forever.

Paul was a rather average size man, much like his son Lee Roy, and they looked so much alike it was uncanny. They even shared some mannerisms. For instance, when either of them wanted to make sure you knew they were being very sharp and slick in their dealings they would wrinkle up their face, give a loud snuff from the side of their mouth and wink real big or nod their head at you.

Leroy Lucas is shown in a recent photograph.

It is sometimes difficult to tell a hard headed person anything and this became apparent to Mickey when he and Lee Roy were students at the old Van Buren High School.

As they tell the tale, one day Lee Roy was standing on a ladder which was leaning against a tree trimming limbs from it as part of a school conservation project.

Mickey tells me that he kept telling Lee Roy to move his ladder. "I kept telling him, Lee Roy you are going to saw that limb off and the ladder will fall," Mickey said.

Lee Roy advised him he knew what he was doing and he kept that handsaw moving. So Mickey backed off, got out of the way and let him keep sawing. He could see that the ladder was leaning against the limb being sawn, but Lee Roy was overlooking the obvious.

Before long, sure enough, the limb was sawed through and indeed the ladder had been leaning on that limb. It fell, as did Lee Roy, breaking some bones in his foot.

Lee Roy Lucas, 1956   *Mickey Ayers, 1956*   *Dave Williamson in*
graduation picture.   *graduation picture.*   *his younger days*

Between the antics of Lee Roy, Mickey and Dave Williamson, the principal of Van Buren High School, Ralph Waldo McCullough, must not have ever seen a dull day. I'll bet he breathed a sigh of relief when those guys graduated in 1956.

Lee Roy was a fast driver, nearly scaring Mickey to death at times. Later, after he had a family, he became leery of even attending a race track. Now he is kind of laid back. He is still actively working for the State of Indiana as a director in the state's Vocational Education training sector. He is a retired automotive instructor for the Kentucky school system and was a paratrooper for the 82nd and 101st airborne during his service years.

Lee Roy Lucas wears his 82nd airborne uniform.

He married and fathered three children, two boys and a girl, and later was divorced. He now is married to Beverly Lucas.

Lee Roy's children, Ronnie, Rhonda and Robbie in 1991.

Lee Roy and his family used to stay away from us sometimes for three years or more at a time while they were living in other states. Then in the middle of the night, we never knew when he was going to come see us but he and his family were always welcome, he would pull into our driveway. To announce his arrival, as soon as he got out of his vehicle he would start shooting his latest big gun, waking everyone in the holler up.

Unlike city folk who might panic if they heard shooting outside their homes, we just got up and admitted the shooter and his family. We would have been greatly surprised to find anyone other than Lee Roy and his family outside. He was our only visitor who announced himself in this manner.

When we moved from the Susie Ayers Road home to Becks Grove in 1978, we had not seen Lee Roy for awhile. I was scared he would pull into our old home place and start shooting and scare the new owner to death or perhaps get shot himself, but that never happened. He told me one time that a family member of his had told him where we had moved to so he knew not to do that again.

When Paul was coming to see us on the Susie Ayers Road we had two big pet white geese that followed every step any of us made when we were outdoors. We could pick these beautiful creatures up and carry them around (if we could lift them after they got so heavy) and pet them to our heart's content. They never offered to peck at us if they were in our arms, but on the ground was another story.

Mickey holds one of our white geese, while Douglas pets it.

If we didn't feed or water them early enough in the morning they would waddle up on the back steps and with their beaks, peck on the patio door until we went out and gave them their corn and fresh water. If I was hanging the wash on the clothesline to dry, one would nonchalantly follow me back and forth. When I was not looking, it would stretch its long neck over and try to bite me on the leg. When I would look down to scold it, the goose would avert its head and look totally innocent and waddle away a few steps. When I went back to hanging wet clothes, back it would come again. I had learned early on that a bite from a full grown goose could be quite painful.

Beginning each year about the first of October, the geese would start laying eggs; each laying an egg every other day. Not thinking about that, we had not provided them with a nesting box so they made their own. Not to be deterred, they used two of the basement window wells and would fill them half full of their huge eggs. Since we had no gander they would not hatch, but the geese did not know that and sat contentedly on those eggs for days at a time. Occasionally we would clean the window wells out but they would just return and use them again and again.

Our boys loved scrambled eggs in the morning for breakfast so I decided to try feeding them some of the goose eggs. One goose egg and one hen egg blended together made just enough scrambled eggs to feed both boys. That worked pretty well until one morning I ran out of hen eggs and just used the goose eggs. If you have ever tried scrambling or frying a goose egg you will know that the whites do not turn truly white as a chicken's egg does, but just goes an opaque color. The boys saw that and would never eat one of them again, but we did use some of them for Easter eggs then fed them to the dogs later.

Everyone in our valley and all the way to Story disliked those geese with a passion. Every time something or someone moved on or near our property, or a car went up or down the road, those two geese would run toward the road with their long necks outstretched, honking loudly, repelling any and all invaders. They were very territorial.

This is one of our beautiful white geese. They were our "watch" geese and alerted us to every movement near our home.

Each evening after school when they saw the big yellow school bus coming, they would run out and greet the boys, honking loudly at them all the way across the yard to the door with them. I guess they were glad to see the boys and their honking had driven that big yellow bus away.

Paul was at our house one day as we were packing to move to Becks Grove and wanted to know what we were going to do with our geese.

We had planned to bring them with us they were such pets, but we didn't have anywhere fenced in to keep them yet. It was too wild where we were moving to just let them run loose because they would not have lasted one night on their own in the woods. Coyotes or foxes would have had a good meal with our pets.

Paul said he would be glad to take Squish and Squirt (obvious names if you know anything about geese at all) home with him and they could swim on his pond. He had a gander but no females and said he had built a goose house by the side of his pond. He said, "When I get some babies hatched I will give you a new start." That sounded reasonable so we let him take our loud friends home with him, but within a couple of months, foxes had caught both of them so we never got a new start.

When Mickey was a very young boy, perhaps three or four years old, he and his Grandma Lizzie were visiting her niece, Dora Kritzer, the wife of Kenneth Kritzer. Dora had some ducks and Mickey fell in love with them. He saw the huge eggs they laid and was intrigued, so Dora gave him one egg for his very own to hatch. Being very careful not to break the egg, he and Grandma returned home with it. Grandma Lizzie had a setting hen at the same time so she slipped the duck egg under the hen to be hatched.

Mickey, like any small boy would do, said he would sit in front of that hen and watch her for hours, waiting for his duck to hatch, until finally, great day in the morning, he was the proud papa of a little fluffy yellow baby duck.

Some people say that ducks and some other fowl will bond with the first person or thing they see when they leave their shell and this little duck bonded with him. Everywhere the kid went, the little duck followed.

Then disaster struck!! Grandma Lizzie needed some things from either the Monday or Thursday peddler and didn't have any money or any produce to trade. She was desperate for the goods she needed so she had to trade Mickey's by now fully grown white duck to the peddler in payment for her merchandise.

The peddler man, as was usual, was happy to take the duck in trade from Grandma Lizzie. He kept wooden cages tied to his wagon for just such events. Then he continued on down the road toward Elkinsville trading with other housewives as he went along the way. Before the peddler left Elkinsville that same day, the duck had been bought by Paul's wife, Violet.

It is just as well that Mickey never found out the fate of his pet duck. It may have ended up as the centerpiece on Violet's Thanksgiving or Christmas table and he would have been mad at the Lucas family the rest of his life. He might have missed out on being friends with Lee Roy, all because of a little duck from their childhood.

This story just shows how the lives of everyone in this small neighborhood were intertwined on a daily basis; not just through marriages and events but through animals such as geese (me and Paul) or even through the hatching of a simple little duckling.

This one little duck connected the Kritzer family (who had the duck that laid the egg); the Wilkerson family (owner of the setting hen); the Ayers family (owner of the hatched duck); the Peddler Man (who traded for the duck); and the Lucas family (the ultimate owner of the little duck).

Then, too, there was Douglas' deal with Bud Fleetwood for the capture of Bud's bantam chickens that I spoke about in another chapter.

In Doug's later years, he and I would nickname one of his friends, Brian Terwedo of Michigan, the Clucker because we figured he was chicken about something or another and Brian wanted his name to appear in this book. Since I am speaking of chickens and other fowl in this chapter it seemed a good place to hide Brian's name and make him look for it.

Paul and Violet are buried in the Duncan Cemetery west of Nashville. Lee Roy lives in Greenwood with his wife Beverly during the week, spending most weekends on his farm in Kentucky.

The Bohall Men

Bohall was the family name of Bill (the father), and Bob, Jesse and Joe, his sons. Bill himself was the son of Josie Bohall, an old time basket weaver in Brown County who was photographed at work weaving baskets and made famous by noted photographer Frank Hohenberger.

About the only thing I can remember about Bill Bohall was that he was a crippled man. Bob told me his dad had polio when he was about 13 years old and that was why he was crippled. I don't recall him ever using a wheelchair, and he was able to drive a car.

When he needed to buy something Bill would drive his car to wherever he needed to go (like to Clothie's), sit outside the building, and blow the horn constantly until someone came outside to see what he wanted. If he needed groceries or gas, Clothie Hedrick would gather them up and put them in his car, or fill his car's tank with gasoline. He would then pay her and drive away.

I don't know how he managed once he got back home to Blue Creek where he lived alone for many years. Perhaps he brought his groceries in by dragging them in a gunny sack or something. For major purchases such as a week's supply of food, another person would purchase and deliver the food to his kitchen, Bob said.

Bill was kind of grumpy most of the time, but I guess I would have been grumpy too if I had been crippled as he was.

We would come to know his son, Bob, best of any of the Bohalls.

In his young days Bob was a really nice looking man with a full head of curly dark hair. But when it became summer time his head would get a buzz cut until the fall. He followed many dreams in his lifetime and served in the military. He has one son Bryan who lives in St. Louis and two grandchildren. Bob is divorced from Betty Bohall of Bloomington but they see each other about twice a month. She still looks out for him, shopping for and bringing him his groceries and medications as needed. Like other couples I have known in this county and others, they get along best when they don't live together.

Loving the idea of flying free as a bird, Bob obtained his pilot's license and worked around airports for awhile. Occasionally Bob would invite Mickey to come to Bloomington where he lived at the time we lived in Copperhead Hollow, and fly with him. They would pool their money, rent a plane and buzz our house and the Story store at a very low altitude.

The boys and I would run outside when we heard that little noisy plane coming overhead. Bob would tilt the plane to one side so we could see Mickey and wave at him. This tickled the boys to death to see their dad flying around. They would make a few passes over us, then head back toward Bloomington waggling the plane's wings at us to say goodbye. What fun they had. This just added more fuel to Lonnie's passion to become a pilot himself which he would do when he was only 15 years old.

As age began to creep up on Bob and infirmities set in, he moved a small camper trailer to his cousin Lowell Bohall's place on Blue Creek Road and settled in for the duration. He has resided in this camper for several years. Though small, it is fully self-contained and provides him with all the necessities for living. He raises a small garden every year and shares what he raises with his neighbors. He even tells where his private crop of morel mushrooms grow and will let best friends pick them.

Bob Bohall's camper home on Blue Creek.

Today he has many afflictions which sometimes keep him from stirring outside his home very much, but he enjoys watching and feeding the area's wildlife and caring for a dog.

At one time Bob drank pretty heavily and smoked cigarettes by the ton. He got really drunk one time and called our house saying he was going to commit suicide. Mickey, knowing how sick Bob had been and believing him capable of suicide to rid himself of pain, rushed the 15 miles down there and found Bob sound asleep and safe in his bed. Mick searched around until he found Bob's pistol, removed the shells and left him sleeping. Bob never knew Mickey was on the place.

Bob Bohall

The next day after this happened I got to thinking about what Bob had done to Mickey, scaring him half out of his wits, and I got madder than a scalded cat. Mickey could have had a serious accident rushing down there to help him.

I telephoned Bob and read him the riot act. I remember telling him that if he ever called us and said that again, that he wouldn't have to commit suicide because I would do the job for him myself. From that day forward Bob stopped drinking.

I told him later, when it became apparent that he really had stopped drinking, that if I had known my yelling threats at him would have made him stop drinking that I would have done it years before. This was the second man I had caused to quit drinking. The first was Ansel Hillenburg. Now there are a couple of others I need to work on.

The same thing happened with his cigarette smoking. Seemed like every week or two he would call me wanting us to pick up some cartons of cigarettes and bring them to him. He always paid us back when we arrived, but it was a pain. He didn't drive much by this time and sometimes it was inconvenient to stop what we were doing and run to the store for him. He wouldn't even try to quit.

By this time I had wised up myself and stopped smoking, and remembering how much good it had done for me to get on Bob about his drinking, I did the same thing with his smoking. He quit smoking too for a long time. I have not visited him for awhile now but I hope he has not started that habit again, but I believe he has restarted. But, if he has restarted smoking, he no longer asks us to pick up his cigarettes.

Although the three brothers are sometimes feuding and yelling at each other they are still family. Jesse lives near Corydon in southern Indiana. Joe has recently moved a small camper for himself to the same property Bob occupies. Bob and Joe might get miffed and cuss and yell at each other occasionally, but so far they have been able to make up and live side by side.

Joe Bohall

Joe enjoys pretty good health and gets around well. He is able to keep an eye on Bob, from a near distance at least. Their place is the last home site on Blue Creek Road. Once you pass their place, the road ends in a creek and the road has now been blocked off.

Even knowing how pretty and quiet their place is it would be a lonely existence if not for the visits of the wildlife in the area.

Bob spends a good deal of his retirement income on cracked corn for the deer, raccoons, possums and waterfowl which visit his place regularly. In the summer he keeps numerous hummingbird feeders filled with sugar water which attracts dozens of these beautiful birds.

Fat and sassy bluejays, cardinals, robins and other colorful song birds flit from tree to tree year around after leaving Bob's well-stocked bird feeders. He has recently been seeing an eagle flying over and swears one picked up a small fawn. After dark it is not unusual to hear the area's coyotes singing to each other. Their homestead is truly a wildlife sanctuary. Perhaps it could better be described as a "brother sanctuary" also?

Joe Bohall's camper home sits on a cousin's property on Blue Creek road.

Scott and Sandra Ayers

Scott is Mick's next younger brother and the former Sandra Lucas is his wife. Sandra was a cousin of Lee Roy Lucas and lived not too far from Lee Roy. We pitched in on labor and helped them build the ranch house in the curve of 135 as it goes through Story in the 1970s. Their daughter Penny Tolle and her family live in that house today. We also assisted them in building a second house on top of a hill off Pension Branch. Gerald was Scott's first name but no one ever called him that except occasionally his wife. They have two daughters, now Penny Tolle and Michelle Crum (she lives on Beck's Grove Road with her family); four grandchildren and three great-grandchildren.

It became a custom, in the 1960s and '70s with several families in the Story community who wanted to build a new house, for the owner to buy the building materials and all the other residents involved in such projects would furnish the labor. That is how Scott, Mickey, his Aunt Ann, cousin Diane Ayers and several other people in the area got new homes built. It was much cheaper all the way around if the labor was donated and allowed us to build the homes fairly quickly with so many helping out.

After graduating high school Scott worked in Columbus, first at Arvin's, later retiring from Cummins Engine Company. Sandra most always was a stay-at-home mom, except for a few years when she waited tables at either the Nashville House or the Story Store.

A family photo of Scott, Sandra, Penny and Michelle Ayers.

Their whole family, ours, and Aunt Ann and her husband Jim Pruitt, spent many wonderful summer evenings sitting along the creek bank fishing in Salt Creek near Stogsdill Hill down past Blue Creek. At that time, even though the road stopped in the creek, we were able to ford it and drive a mile or so further to this favorite fishing hole. You cannot get there now because someone blocked access to prevent anyone from using the road. In her youth, Sandra had lived just beyond where the present road ends.

On those evenings we spent fishing, we would load everyone into the back of a pickup truck along with enough food to feed an army and all our fishing equipment and baits and head out. Sometimes there were so many going fishing, we needed two vehicles.

Sandra or I nearly always would have a cake or pie baked. We would take hotdogs, hamburger meat, buns, bread, marshmallows, chips and condiments along with soft drinks for the kids and maybe a brewskie or two for the guys and several pieces of long-burning heavy wood for the fire. We provided the food; the guys supplied the yucky worms for bait, removed fish from the poles and baited our hooks when necessary. In my opinion this was a fair trade since I will not touch a nasty worm. I cannot abide one of the slithery things twining around my fingers as I try to bait my own hook. That job is for men or young kids you can coerce into doing the job in exchange for another marshmallow or something like that.

Once we arrived at the old fishing hole the first order of business was to bait up all the poles and drop the lines into the water. Next would come gathering enough dry twigs to get a bonfire going over which the hotdogs, hamburgers and marshmallows would be cooked. This was a fun job for the kids and it only took those energetic youngsters a few minutes to gather enough to start a fire. One of the guys with a sharp knife would be dispatched to cut some green roasting sticks. Everything had to be gathered before it got dark so no one would step off into the creek and be hurt.

I really think we ate more than we fished, but it didn't matter. What really mattered was that three generations of one family were spending time together as a family and it was always an enjoyable time with much teasing.

Many fish stories would be told by the guys with a lot of "I don't believe that" heard from the kids.

Michelle was only about four or five years old when we went there one evening. She had been fishing for awhile and catching some pretty nice yellow bellies (small catfish), when suddenly her pole went down and she almost fell into the water. That scared this little tomboy nearly to death. She had never hooked up with such a big fish before.

Scott grabbed her and helped get the fish up onto the bank. It was a big carp, probably six or eight pounds at least, for a little girl that size to catch, and she wanted nothing to do with that big ugly fish. We brought it home with us and took her picture but she would not touch that fish even to have her picture taken.

At other times, especially in early spring when the suckers were running, you could find our families along another bank of Salt Creek east of Story near Dave Williamson's place. A sucker is a rough fish, akin to the carp family, though those that ate them said they tasted much better than a carp if fixed right.

Mickey peers into the murky water waiting for a sucker he could snare.

There were three varieties of suckers, the Redhorse, Blackhorse and Whitehorse. For eating purposes, most people preferred the Blackhorse because it had small scales and had a slightly more delicate flavor. The other varieties had large rounded rough scales and looked much more like a carp than the black did.

To eat a sucker you first had to "score" them. This meant that once gutted and halved lengthwise, you scored or cut through the meaty side about every eighth of an inch or so to disable the bones which were coarse and numerous. They could then be dipped in an egg batter and deep fried. These fish were a good source of cheap protein for the people of this area for many years during some very hard times. As times improved they didn't need the protein source so much but they still enjoyed the sport so much it continued for many years.

The guys in earlier times used a gig to catch these fish. A gig was a tool, usually having from three to five very sharp barbed tines about three inches long, affixed to a long pole. It was deadly and accurate. Two or three men working together could spear a lot of fish in just one outing.

They would go out after dark, either holding a powerful flashlight in one hand or mounting a light on their caps, to enable them to see the fish beneath the water. When they spotted one of these suckers going up onto a riffle (a gravelly area of the creek covered with swiftly flowing shallow water) to spawn, they would use the gig to stab the fish and retrieve it.

This could be difficult to do even with a bright light because water distorts images and the fish were sometimes missed. Time would be wasted waiting for them to settle down again. Once the sucker was on the gig's end, it could then be removed and placed into a gunny sack which was slung over the backs of the men by means of a sling.

In later years, after the practice of gigging became illegal, the guys determined that they could snare the fish in a noose just as easily, and for the most part, this was a legal means for taking the fish. At least it was legal in certain areas, including the area of Salt Creek flowing where we lived.

A snare was made by attaching a copper noose to a long cane pole by means of a heavy venetian blind cord or other heavy twine. Copper wire was used for the noose because it was easily visible under water. To hold it down under the water once the noose was opened, a heavy nut or round stone with a hole in the center was attached for better control of the noose wire.

When a sucker was sighted, the person holding the cane pole would lean out over the water, placing the loop of the noose either just before or just behind the fish, whichever they preferred so long as it did not touch the fish; working it over the body to just behind the fish's head. When it was in this position, the pole would be yanked hard, the fish captured and it could then be thrown to the handlers on the creek bank. The fish would be removed, the noose reopened and returned to the man with the pole ready for the next use.

This activity could only be done in the spring of each year when the fish were moving upstream to spawn. Usually the season lasted only a few days because, as was usual in the spring, a rain would fall and roil the water, making it impossible to see the fish and also raising the water level in the creek. But while the water was clear and shallow, a lot of fish could be snared. The spawning could continue during this high water time, but we could not see it happening so our "fishing" would be over for another year.

It was common when this was practiced to see a line of cars parked along the roadway and men and women staring down into the creek. They were watching to see if they could see these fish moving. If they spotted them moving upstream, word was sent out to all the neighbors and poles would be readied for the next day's fishing.

One year those gathered around the banks took at least a half ton of fish from the same hole in the creek. All were eaten, traded for other things, given away to the area's widows if they wanted a fish or two or frozen for later use. None went to waste.

Scott, Doug and Mick, hold part of a day's catch of fish.

It seems like sometimes when the guys doing the snaring swung the fish toward the banks that they were trying to slap someone with them. Those females were loaded with eggs and when they hit you or landed on the creek bank, those ripe eggs would fly out and by days end you would be covered with the nasty deep orange things.

Those eggs, usually removed when the fish were cleaned, might be rinsed, rolled in a fish batter and deep fried along with the meat to be eaten as a spring delicacy. I never enjoyed eating either the fish or the roe so I rarely ate any of this, but the others enjoyed the treat and we would have well-attended fish fry's with many side dishes and desserts. There might be two or more dozen relatives and friends attend one of our fish fry's which were normally held at Scott and Sandra's place.

Sandra also was the woman on call if one of our boys got hurt or sick in school. There were many times while I was at work that I got a call from her stating, "Meet me at the hospital." One or the other of our boys would need medical attention. I would drop whatever I was doing and head towards Columbus to retrieve my kid. Usually by the time I got there they had stitches, bandages or casts already applied and would be ready to be picked up, taken home and put to bed.

Several years after we finished their Story house, Scott and Sandra moved to another new one we had helped them build atop a hill off Pension Branch, just south of Story. That corner in Story where their first home stood has been in the Ayers family inventory of homes for many, many years.

Mickey was born there in a log cabin that burned during WW II when he was young. Grandma Lizzie used the space for a garden for many years. Scott and Sandra built a house there; then it was sold to Scott's parents and now Scott owns it again, and allows their daughter Penny to live there. Ownership of this lot just goes around and around in a circle. Now it is the only home in Story that is not included in the bed and breakfast operation next door.

When Mickey was about six or seven years old his family was living in that log house and his dad was serving on Okinawa fighting the Japanese. Not wanting to be outdone, Mickey took a wooden beer box up on the roof of that house, climbed inside his "airplane" and prepared to fight the "Japs" that he had heard the family say his dad was fighting. He learned a very valuable lesson that day. He learned that a silk scarf did not make a very substantial parachute when you bailed out of a beer box airplane. He hit the ground very hard when his "plane" slid off that metal roof down to the hard ground.

When Penny was a girl growing up she was crazy about motorcycles. Beginning with a small 50 cc engine when she was very young, she progressively moved up in engine size bikes until now she rides a full size Harley Davidson motorcycle. The lot where this house is situated was only a pie-shaped three-quarter acres, but Penny rode those motorcycles of hers around that pie shape area several thousands of miles. I don't know if she kept track of how many miles were put on each machine, but it had to be lots and lots.

Sandra was also the aunt of our boys who liked to bake cookies, usually baking them two or three times every week. One bad winter, I believe it was the snowy one of 1976-77, she started baking peanut butter cookies. She was generous and shared the results with Douglas every time she baked. This started about Christmas time that winter and continued on into February. Each time Douglas ate some of the cookies he would wake up the following morning with a few red spots on his chest and belly. Each time he broke out there were more spots than the last time.

Since I never could make cookies that looked like anything, I had convinced my boys that only their aunt Sandra and the Keebler elves knew how to bake them. For years they believed this to be true.

One day Douglas decided to bake some cookies himself. Using the recipe Sandra gave him he made a double batch of peanut butter cookies and within a day or so had eaten every one of them. The next morning he woke up with the worst case of hives I have every seen. I took him to Dr. Robert Seibel in Nashville and he told me he had to be eating something that he was allergic to and I would have to figure out what it was.

Returning home with some medication for Doug to relieve his itching we got to thinking about what he could be eating that was new to his diet that he was reacting to. The only thing that came to mind was peanut butter so we called the doctor and he agreed that many people were allergic to nuts and Doug was most likely one of those people. Sure enough, he stopped eating peanut butter and never got the hives again.

At the present time, Scott and Sandra are living near Seymour along the banks of White River where they can be seen skimming along the river in their air boat, fishing on a daily basis. That is some kind of retirement.

Keith Donaldson

Keith Donaldson was another of those people for whom no history of Van Buren would be complete without a few words being written about him. For many years he served as the county's Democratic Party chairman. His wife Kay would work just as diligently with Orville and Olivia Toler for the Republican Party, much to Keith's chagrin. This political arrangement was very similar to the one my parents enjoyed and it worked for both couples except on election days. The vote of one half of each couple would cancel the vote of the other half as each followed their party lines when they voted.

A very young and quite handsome Keith Donaldson.

Kay Donaldson not long before she passed away.

After we moved to the Becks Grove community, Keith and Kay were our next door neighbors to the north. I have previously written about the Tolers in another chapter; they were the township's two hottest Republicans. Keith was the red-hottest Democrat by far. Others may have been staunch Democrats, but Keith was absolutely rabid about it.

During election years he could be heard to say to anyone within hearing distance at the polls that it never took him more than five seconds to vote. Pull one lever or mark one place on the paper ballot and he was done voting, he loudly bragged.

Keith and Kay had lived on the family homestead next to us for many years. His farm consisted of about 160 acres, used more recently as hay fields that he could sell and/or rent out to another farmer.

He also had a side-line business of restoring antique furniture and was in great demand all over the county for those talents. Many of the antiques in Brown County homes today were restored by the artistic hands of Keith Donaldson.

Four generations of the Donaldson men. From left; Alan, Keith holding Alan's son Mark, and Keith's father, D. C. Donaldson.

Keith moved to Brown County in 1935 and lived here until his death in 1995. His father came here from Maywood, IL in 1955 onto a 40 acre farm where the Brown Park Lake is now located on Keith Donaldson Road.

Keith was first married to Dorothy Schrougham and they had two children, Alan and Janet. After Dorothy died, he then married Kathryn Neat and she preceded Keith in death from a battle with cancer.

Dorothy Donaldson sits on her front porch swing enjoying some time with her young daughter, Janet. Dorothy died of cancer in 1961.

Keith would tell everyone how hard things had been for his family during the Great Depression of the '30s and during the war years.

"We lived on green beans," he would relate. "One winter that was what we had to eat, three meals every day. I will never eat another green bean as long as I live," and, if we were outside when he said that, he would spit as though to get the taste out of his mouth again.

He really wouldn't either. During Democrat Party functions, if he was served a meal that included green beans, he would send his plate back to the kitchen and demand that the cook make up another completely new plate for him. He didn't want even the smell of green beans remaining on his plate.

Because of that he would never plant a green bean in his big garden. He planted enough of everything else that he could share with us and many others freely, but no matter how much I begged him, he would not plant any green beans. Deer continued to eat down my green bean plants so we were never very successful in raising this crop and I loved green beans with the same passion that Keith hated them.

One year though he did plant some sugar snap peas which, when he shared them with me, turned out to be just as good if not better than green beans and he welcomed me to come to his garden and pick all I wanted, and I did so. They were delicious.

He called me down to his place one day to see his zucchini plants. "One is a monster from outer space," he told me.

When I arrived he showed me a plant that was unbelievable in size. The plant spread out for at least eight feet in all directions and stood up about three feet tall and had dozens of zucchinis of all sizes attached. Both he and Kay and my family ate zucchini that summer in as many ways as we could determine to fix them. I became almost as sick of zucchini as he was of green beans, but he kept foisting them off on me to get rid of them. I think he finally just chopped the plant down.

For many years it was a joke around the county, that if you drove your car to Nashville in the summer time, you had best lock it up. If you didn't, when you returned to it you might find the entire back seat had been filled with this zucchini squash that a friend had picked from his own garden and shared with you. He would gladly share them with you so they didn't go to waste.

When I threw my hat into the political ring in 1976, I became much better acquainted with Keith and others in the Democratic Party. To Keith there was not a single good Republican, living or dead. In his book only Democrats were worth spit.

Up to that time I had not been active politically, but had decided to celebrate the nation's bi-centennial by running for the office of county commissioner. I had no party backing and I worked very hard in my attempt to win. Even though I lost I must certainly have scared the old-time politicians like Keith to death when I won four of the twelve precincts in the county. I even pulled more votes than another old-time candidate who, although 83 himself, referred to me as "that old Ayers woman." I was only 35 years old at the time I ran.

The man who won that election would tell me a few years down the road that he wished I could have won it. "You would have made a good commissioner," he told me, however little good that sentiment did me by then. Anyway, five days after the 1976 spring primary, I was asked to become the secretary of the county's Democratic Party. I accepted and would hold that position for seven years until I just could not stand to hear how bad and awful the Republicans were. I knew several Republicans by this time and they were not of another species or bad people at all, maybe misdirected is all. I am beginning to sound just like Keith.

Two years after I ran for county commissioner I again ran for a county office—the office of auditor—at the urging of the Democrat Party chiefs. The party backed me 100 percent this time and I won the election hands down; however I never served as auditor. My editor, Greg Temple, asked me to remain at the newspaper and serve my county through the printed word, and that's just what I did.

This permitted the county politicians to choose another good Democrat to serve in my stead so it all worked out pretty well in the end.

Greg once wrote an editorial about "Yellow Dog Democrats." Keith took that description so to heart that he immediately canceled his long-held subscription to the newspaper and would never allow a copy of it to come into his home again. If Kay wanted to read it, she had to read it while at work, while visiting the library or while visiting a friend's house. He would allow me to visit him in his home even though I worked at this despicable place, but I could not sneak a copy of the paper in for Kay to read.

When the editorial was written it was an election year and Greg had been describing how some people would vote for a yellow dog running for office as long as it was running on the Democrat ticket before they would vote for a Republican, thereby the term, "Yellow Dog Democrat."

For many years during elections, the Tolers would see the tallies from Van Buren Township showing hundreds of Democrat votes cast along with two or three Republican ballots. A big year might see six or seven Republican votes cast here, but they continued to persevere. Nowadays there are many Republicans living in Brown County; but Van Buren Township continues to be a Democratic stronghold, for the time being at least.

An older version of Keith Donaldson. He was this age when I knew him.

The old time politicians such as Keith always said when a Republican could win the majority of the votes in Van Buren Township it would be a sad day indeed. I believe the Republicans have held a majority of county offices perhaps only three times in our history, but the influx of newcomers shows that more and more of them are Republicans so the chances of it happening are much greater now.

The days of Keith Donaldson type politics may be at an end. In the older days of our history one could be elected to a county wide office merely on the strength of the family name alone. You didn't have to be qualified in any other manner to hold an office. Those days, too, are behind us I believe.

To Keith, no matter how well he knew the individual or admired them professionally and personally on a daily basis, if they were a Republican, he had no use for them at election time.

"There ain't a good one among 'em," he could be heard to scoff.

Both Keith and Kay are now dead. His son and daughter, Alan and Janet, operate the old homestead as a bed and breakfast business, and the days of old time politics are now also almost gone.

Amos and Olive Wilkerson

Amos, now 83 years young, is Mickey's uncle. He is the son of the late Grover and Lizzie Wilkerson and grew up in the Story community.

Amos is married to Olive Moore Wilkerson who hails from the same Jackson County town of Kurtz in which I grew up. I didn't know Olive when she lived at Kurtz. I was much younger than her. She had married and moved to Brown County long before I became acquainted with her.

This couple would play a part in my wedding. My mother had been planning a big church wedding for us and I just could not face going through all the preparations and spending so much of my hard earned money, so one cold day in March 1960, Mickey and I eloped, taking Amos and Olive with us. We drove to the Baptist Church in Seymour and asked the minister to marry us.

During our fourteen month courtship we spent many dates with Amos and Olive at their home near Spurgeon's Corner. We were saving as much money as we possibly could so we could set up a household when we married so we spent many evening at their home enjoying their company to save money.

It was a good thing they went with us when we eloped because Amos nearly had to hold Mickey erect he was so scared. I always teased Mickey that he wasn't afraid of getting married, but was scared of what my dad would say. Both my parents liked Mickey and accepted the fact that there would be no big wedding for us.

Amos Wilkerson   *Olive Wilkerson*

Olive loves to dance three or four nights every week. She keeps Amos on the move driving her to various places to enjoy the music which she has enjoyed her entire life. I sometimes tease her that it doesn't matter if the band members can sing or not as long as they are loud and the band can produce a dance beat.

I have seen her dance every dance for three or four hours straight two or three times each week and she is constantly cajoling others sitting along the sidelines to join her.

About three years ago she and Amos and her sister Laverne Williams were in a near-fatal auto accident in Bartholomew County. Olive received some substantial injuries including a broken arm. For a few weeks after she was released from the hospital she wore one arm in a cast and sling when she attended gatherings where music was played.

She did not dance for awhile and it seemed she had forgotten that she loved music so much. That cast came off and less than a month later she lost her balance and broke the other arm which was casted and put in a sling.

As she got progressively healthier except for the arm in a sling, she remembered how much she liked to dance. After that, even though she was still bruised and battered and had an arm in a sling, she began dancing again and continues to do so.

I guess that is what makes her so strong today at the ripe age of 81. She will never stop dancing.

Grandma Lizzie always said that Olive was a hypochondriac and that may be correct. She spends as much time at doctor's offices and emergency rooms as other people have spent working for a living. But I am not a doctor so I cannot say for sure that she imagines her illnesses.

Olive Wilkerson in her much younger days.

A year or so ago the doctor prescribed her a very expensive medication that was supposed to delay the onset and debilitation of the mind in old age. She was telling me that she had put the pills away. "I can still cook and go to the bathroom by myself," she said. "Why do I need memory pills?"

That was a good question. I asked her what she did with the memory pills and after studying the question for a few minutes said, "You know, I don't remember where I put them."

That explains Olive very well I think.

Jose and Lucinda Vasquez

Jose (Joe to his friends) and his wife Chinda (Lucinda) arrived in Brown County from southwest Texas in 1961 and settled in near the old Van Buren School on Christiansburg Road with their two daughters and four sons.

Joe came to Brown County to raise Christmas trees for the commercial tree markets. He, his family members, and many other migrant workers toiled endlessly in the hot sticky fields of pine trees, trimming and shaping, weeding and mowing, re-setting new trees after the harvest was completed. There was never a slow day for the hard-working Vasquez family.

Jose and Chinda Vasquez at their 50th Wedding Anniversary.

Upon his arrival Joe at first worked for others. Over time he was able to accumulate some pretty poor agricultural land that would be ideal for growing Christmas trees and went to work for himself. Joe told me one time that the best places to grow the trees was in the gently rolling land along the undulating ridges of southern Van Buren Township.

Over the years the land had been farmed nearly to ruin, and then allowed to erode. His planting of the fast growing Christmas trees prevented a lot of erosion and gave many people a job. Prior to Joe's arrival on the scene, several others had planted Christmas trees to not only bring forth a crop, but to stop erosion. Many local high school students in the 1950s and 1960s were hired by other tree farmers such as Don Goodwin and Greg Ransburg to plant thousands of trees.

But, unlike Joe's trees, many of these trees were not intended for the market and over the next several years there developed many acres of over-grown Christmas trees that were generally not good for much of anything commercially. They were allowed to grow unmolested to protect the soil but they would be a bear to clear for better tended crops at a later date. As they aged they became brittle and every wind storm would see many of these dying trees broken over creating windfalls. I'm sure a lot of wildlife liked the trees, but someone trying to clear them for a different use of the land would become frustrated. We own one such 40 acre plot of these overgrown trees and it is a real mess but Mickey is making progress on cleaning it up.

This is not to say that a few growers were not successful here before Joe arrived because Don Goodwin also was successful raising the trees. He depended upon a Mexican labor force to a great extent though to harvest his crops.

One of the first things Joe did with any newly arriving field hands was to take them to Dr. Robert Seibel in Nashville and get them inoculated with the poison ivy serum. They proved to be as highly allergic to this weed as I. One day I was there getting my shots when a whole big group of Mexicans got in line behind me for theirs. These shots help prevent the worst of the itchy rash and these workers would be constantly exposed to the noxious weed.

Joe's children were enrolled in the local school system and, for the most part, were well liked and respected members of their classes. All the Vasquez children are bi-lingual adults today. Their sons participated in school sports. Sami played on the Van Buren Mets baseball team with our sons.

I don't believe I could find better neighbors than the Mexicans who live around me. They are exceptionally good neighbors, always ready to lend a hand with any chore, or give readily if one is in need. I know without a doubt I could knock on any of their doors and ask one to help me and without hesitation, they would do so.

I love to attend their fandangos and parties. The women are excellent cooks and they always prepare all their own food for the parties I am invited to attend. My food is almost bland compared to theirs and I have a huge spice cabinet in my kitchen. One of Joe's brothers once brought us some homemade chili he had made. I wouldn't even taste it because when looking into the quart jar you could see hundreds of jalapeño seeds floating in that chili. I know it would have set me on fire had I tasted it, but Mickey loved it and ate the whole jar.

For Joe and Chinda's golden wedding anniversary party, they rented the National Guard Armory in Columbus. There was a huge crowd, Mexican and locals, who attended and danced to the sounds of the mariachi band they had hired. We had an absolutely wonderful time.

I told Joe later about a dish I tried and he laughed at me. I love burritos and they had prepared all the makings I needed to assemble my own. There were two kinds of hot peppers in separate bowls that had been ground very fine. One bowl contained green peppers and one contained red. I, thinking that the green might not be quite as hot as the red, carefully spooned one of those little plastic spoons of the green peppers over my entire burrito then rolled it up ready to eat.

The first bite I swallowed set up such a reaction in me that it nearly knocked me off my chair. My face immediately started sweating behind my glasses and below my nose. My glasses actually steamed up from the heat off that one little bite of hot peppers. And, the Mexicans were spreading tons of that stuff on their food.

Joe laughed when I told him about it later and said, "Oh, gee, you ate the Gringo peppers, you should have tried the kind we like to eat," as he slapped his leg in glee. Any hotter, and I think I would have expired on the spot or at least have been able to blow blue smoke out my ears. Wow!

270 Helen C. Ayers

In the early days of our acquaintance, Joe saw the boys and me alongside the road in a ditch. We had started out that morning to come from Story to our new place at Becks Grove to work on our driveway when I had slid into a ditch. Joe hooked his big 4-wheel drive pick-up truck to my car and pulled me out of the ditch.

After we got to our new place I slid off again into the soft mud along the new driveway we were cutting the brush from. Joe drove by, saw my predicament and pulled me out once again. He told me to go home and stay home until the roads got a little better. He definitely was smarter than I had been. I took his advice and went home.

Another time he helped me out of a pickle. I had bought an older home at a sheriff's sale that needed a lot of work and cleanup. He drove by one day while my nephew and I were working and seeing big piles of dirt lying all over the yard that the previous owner had piled up he said he was going to go home and get his tractor. A little while later he came back with a huge tractor and knocked down every bump and pile and smoothed them out for me.

One part of the land package for that house was very rutted and overgrown. He told me, "I'm gonna go put my plow on now and come and plow that place up for you."

Chinda was with him when he returned that time and she told him after it was finished it was still too rough for me to do anything with and made him drive back home and put the big disk on and disk the dirt smooth.

Driving back to their home from mine and returning was about a ten mile round trip, but that didn't matter to Joe. I needed help and he was willing to provide it without my even asking. They would not take one cent for their work. Now that is neighborliness.

Our oldest son, Lonnie, is married to a girl from Spain and he and their children are bi-lingual. His son, Victor, was visiting me one time and we saw Joe eating watermelon on his front porch. We stopped and Joe gave each of us a slice to enjoy and Victor surprised Joe by talking to him in perfect Spanish.

While my nephew was helping me clean up this old house Joe stopped by, saw Joey and immediately started spouting Spanish at him. Joey looked at me with a question on his face. I told Joe that he was speaking Spanish to the wrong fellow and explained that this kid was young Joseph (Joey), not Victor. The two boys looked a lot alike and were nearly identical in age, but Joey could not speak a word of Spanish.

Joe's sister-in-law, Victoria Guzman, grabbed me and hugged me while we were talking together one day when I was able to speak a phrase or two of Spanish to her. "Oh, you are learning to speak like us," she gushed. She actually understood me!

I had taken a conversational Spanish course over at the high school at the urging of my granddaughter, Mercedes. She had told me when she was four that I should learn to speak a few words of Spanish since I had two Spanish speaking grandchildren, and she was right, so I did and I can.

One of the Vasquez sons, Manual, died suddenly of a cerebral hemorrhage when he was 21. He is buried in the Christiansburg Cemetery. Their son Sami, along with Sam's wife Barbara (Henderson), now is the boss of the Vasquez enterprises. Raymond and Rick live nearby. Their daughter Ana Facundo lives next door to Sami on Keith Donaldson Road and their daughter Lucy lives in Kentucky.

Sami and Barbara Vasquez

The Vasquez family has been a wonderful asset to Van Buren Township. Who says we all have to be cut from the same bolt of cloth to fit into this big old world?

Doc Beauchamp

Finally we come full circle of my favorite people to Doc Beauchamp. Adolph was his real name but I don't recall ever once using that name when I addressed him. He was always just Doc.

Doc and his wife, Hesper ("Hep"Anthony), lived away from Brown County during their working years then they returned to Hep's mother's place at the junction of Gravel Creek and Elkinsville Roads and lived there awhile when Doc retired. Then they moved east to Pike's Peak and lived there the remainder of their lives.

My good friend and buddy, Doc Beauchamp. He was an all around winner in my book.

These two people were like grandparents to me. I loved both of them equally and enjoyed their company as often as I could arrange it. They never minded my just dropping in for a brief visit or a longer one in which we would drag out boxes of their old family pictures. We spent many a wintry afternoon looking at these old photographs.

Hep's mother was Pauline Anthony who claimed Mickey as her grandson when she attended Lenore at his birth. I wrote earlier about Pauline in Grandma Lizzie's story.

Hep was a nurse and worked at her profession right up into her golden years. When Doc retired from his job and moved back to Brown County, he took an active interest in children. For several years he was the coach and/or assistant coach of the Van Buren Mets baseball team, leading it to several county championships.

There wasn't a kid on his team that didn't admire and look up to Doc. He played every player fairly and demanded they respect the less experienced teams they played. Once he took our lead pitcher out of the game because when the other team was up at bat, the boy heckled the other team so badly. Our team was playing a very inexperienced team from Gnaw Bone that evening and at the bottom of the third or fourth inning we were ahead 62-0. Our little pitcher kept mouthing off. Doc finally put him on the side lines as punishment.

If Doc asked the boys a question he expected an honest answer. If he caught them in a lie or an avoidance of answering they would be side lined. He was strict with the young boys but he was extremely fair also.

There were so many admirable qualities about Doc that it would be hard to remember them all.

I made over him and he made over me every time we saw each other. This was OK with Hep because she knew that neither of us meant a thing by it. We just simply admired and liked each other.

After Hep died, Doc continued to be friends with me and my family members.

At that time I had been writing "send-offs" for anyone I knew who had died. The newspaper ran them on the editorial page and everyone loved them. In these articles I wrote about my friends who had died I was permitted to add details that normally would not have been included in an ordinary obituary, but which better described the lives of the deceased. I wrote many of them over the years telling how each of them had touched me and how much knowing them meant to me.

Doc asked me many times to write his send-off before he died. "I want to read what you have to say about me," he would laugh.

I tried to explain that I could not do that because it took their deaths usually to make my brain kick in with what I wanted to say but I guaranteed him I would only say good things about him.

I stopped by his house one day to shoot the breeze with him. Driving by his house I had seen him outside placing wood into a stack. His next door neighbor, Jim Wilkerson, was leaning over the white board fence between the two properties when I arrived. Jim who was of a similar age as Doc was jeering at Doc telling him how much more wood he could split than Doc and Doc was asking him to jump over the fence and show him.

*Jim and Radia Wilkerson, at home in Pike's Peak. Notice
how many items were displayed in their living room. This
was a common practice of many families, however every
single item had to do with their family which created a warm
fuzzy feeling when family and friends came to visit.*

I can just see it now, these two eighty-something old men having
a wood chopping contest.

Jim was the brother of Susie Ayers, Sharlot Fleetwood, Goldie
Williamson, and Agnes Hedrick. I believe there were more children
in this family, but those are the ones I knew about. He married Radia
Ogle.

Doc's friend and good buddy, Jim Wilkerson.

When Jim had seen me coming up behind Doc at various times and putting my arms around his neck and hugging him he told me he wanted to be hugged too so the next time I came up behind the two of them I hugged both from behind. Usually I would see them seated around a table at the Van Buren School functions. But Jim's wife, Radia, didn't like my hugging Jim at all. She told me once, her eyes snapping angrily, "You better be careful about who you hug like that." I really think she was jealous so I had to stop hugging Jim.

One of the last times I saw Doc I was driving into Pike's Peak from Nashville and saw him and a young boy who was maybe nine or ten years old, in the roadway there in front of Eleanor Clark's old store. The boy was holding Doc's hand and letting him ride on a skateboard. I nearly had a stroke.

I quickly parked my car and got out and grabbed Doc's hand and made him get off that thing. I could just image his brittle old bones sounding like breaking twigs if he fell off that contraption.

He put his arm across that young boy's shoulder and told him I was the mother of the two boys he was always telling him about.

That kid asked me if my kids were really as good as Doc was always telling him they were. Since I didn't know what Doc had told him, I just said they were awfully good boys.

Doc assured this young man that my boys were two of the finest boys to ever come out of Brown County.

Gee, Doc, I'm blushing. Wish I could give you another hug.

The Kritzer Families

I have only briefly mentioned the Kritzer family members in previous chapters, so I guess I should elaborate on this family a little bit more.

Ollie was the matriarch of the family. A long ago divorced woman, she lived with her daughter Thelma (Sis) Carmichael and Sis's husband Lee Carmichael.

Ollie Kritzer

The Carmichaels had two daughters and three sons and lived east of Story just past the Mt. Zion Cemetery. The two youngest boys, David and Donnie, were identical mirror twins.

These boys played on the Mets baseball team with our boys, but were slightly younger than ours. One of them broke an arm and we thought, well, now we can surely tell them apart. Less than a week later, the other twin broke the same arm.

Sis (Thelma) and Lee Carmichael and their children except for daughter Pam. Twins David and Donnie, son Danny and daughter, Julie.

Other members of Ollie's clan include her son, Kenneth and his wife Dora Kritzer. Dora was the niece of our Grandma Lizzie. Dora was a homemaker and Kenneth was a minister, school board member for many years and a farmer. He would make a hit with my husband when Mickey was near death in an Indianapolis hospital awaiting first ever of its kind heart surgery. He was lying in bed one evening when in walked Kenneth to visit and pray with him before Mick's surgery the next morning.

Reverend Kenneth Kritzer prayed for my husband's recovery.

My husband was never obviously devout, but he had always been a believer. Kenneth prayed for his recovery. Mickey lived and thrived and returned home where Kenneth visited again and offered more prayers. Mickey has enjoyed many years of quality living since that long ago day August 26, 1968. He has several times told me how much he appreciated Kenneth coming to pray for him.

Kenneth was also a big farmer and he and his son B.J. farmed several hundred acres near Story. Kenneth and Dora also had a daughter, Marsha, but I never knew her.

Kenneth and Dora Kritzer.

Ollie's other son was Rex Kritzer and his wife was named Sarah Louise. They enjoyed a blended family. Rex was the life-long lawman of the family. I think it was 30 years he served as a game warden, later to be called conservation officer, then upon his retirement from that profession he served eight years as Sheriff of Brown County. Their house was on east up the road from the Carmichael place toward Stone Head just beyond Louis and Mabel Henderson's place.

Rex Kritzer, conservation officer, sheriff, farmer and friend.

Rex and his family also farmed hundreds of acres and for many years raised hogs for the market. It was on this farm while he was picking corn one year in the early 1950's that he lost an arm to a corn picker. He told me once how when he was caught in the picker he had to use his pocket knife and cut the remaining bit of his arm off to free his body from the machine or face bleeding to death. He used his belt to make a tourniquet.

For the rest of his life he lived with an artificial arm with a hook for a hand. He became very adept at using the hook and I have seen him writing with a pen clutched in the jaws of the hook many times while he was sheriff. He never appeared self conscious of having a hook and just went on about his business, perhaps never realizing what an accomplishment this actually was.

Early Brown County
Park Officer

This is a George Bredewater rendition of a Brown County Game Warden, now referred to as a Conservation Officer.

He served his two terms as sheriff while I was working at the Brown County Democrat. Many times over the years he and I went at it tooth and toenail as I tried to get stories from him. He could be just as stubborn as I could be so we often locked horns over issues. This did not in any way detract from our admiration for the others' skills. When all was said and done we remained friends.

His sister, Thelma, was the most indomitable woman I ever met. Every day of her life Sis rose early and went to bed late. In between those hours she went at a fast trot and never stopped. She could do the work of at least two normal men and was a devout Christian woman.

Our house burned to the ground in 1963 and we lost everything we had except for a few items. Mickey's dad permitted us to move into one of his homes south of Story. Within three days Sis had made two trips to our house with their big farm truck filled to the brim with household items, soft goods, furniture and food.

After three days the only thing we lacked was a baby bed and a kitchen table, both of which were given to me by the man I had been interviewing with for a job while the house had been afire. (By the way, I also got the job.)

Her efforts on our behalf were incredible. I hardly knew anyone in the area yet by that time in our marriage, but they evidently knew Mickey really well and cared about all of us. We received enough new items such as sheets, blankets and towels from our neighbors to last us for over twenty years.

It wasn't just my family she helped in this way. She willingly did it for anyone needing her assistance and she never had to be asked. She was the instigator of willing assistance.

When her twins were only nine months old she discovered she had breast cancer. She underwent chemotherapy and for the next nine years was adjudged to be cancer-free. Then with a vengeance, the cancer returned and within two months, Sis was dead.

What a loss to the neighborhood the deaths of all the Kritzer elders have been. Sarah Louise is the lone survivor as I write.

Gary and Judy Huffman

What can you say about a man who looks enough like your husband to be a twin brother to him, yet is not related, but is instead your husband's best friend?

Mickey and Gary met not long after Gary returned from his fourth tour of Viet Nam. Mickey was a deputy sheriff in Brown County at the time they met and their mutual appreciation for each other led to their becoming best friends.

Gary made four tours to the war torn country of Viet Nam and was injured four times. I told him maybe he should have thought about the second and subsequent tours, but I believe he would offer to go back again today if anyone asked him to. Once a Marine, always a Marine. Semper fi.

Originally from a law enforcement family in Cincinnati and its environs, he served Brown County and the state of Indiana as a deputy sheriff and conservation officer for many years. He then returned to Cincinnati and served on the police force there at the North College Hill precinct until a drunk driver ran into his patrol car and broke Gary's neck, forcing him into an early retirement. At one time he and two of his brothers were policemen in Cincinnati.

Once he retired he moved back to Brown County and bought eight acres from the south end of our farm. Mickey and he built his home that he shares with his wife, Judy. They have an adult daughter, Holly, and she and her husband Mike have three daughters. He owns a fishing charter business on Lake Michigan that he continues to operate today.

It is this fishing business that I would like to talk about. For many years after he bought the business he and Mickey would go up there and fish, bringing home enormous amounts of salmon. He loves fish as does my husband. I can't stand the smell of the stuff but I love to fish so I begged them to take me with them the next time they went.

They finally agreed to take me but I could not find any seasick medicine before I left. I spent the entire trip hanging limply over the gunwale chumming the fishes. Every time I became able to look up from the water I would see these two jokers eating stinking salami sandwiches with raw onions or drinking a beer. The sight and smell of those stinky sandwiches would just send me right back to the rail. At the end of the first day another boat captain who was having supper with us gave me a patch to place on the bone behind my ear. The next day I was able to fish, but we ran into other problems.

We usually left for Lake Michigan about 1 or 2 o'clock in the morning and went directly to the boat about daylight. We had been fishing the first day with no problem other than my stomach. The second day Gary lay down to take a nap and left Mickey to run the boat. All we had to do was steer it and pull in a fish if one got on our lines. That sounds pretty simple and actually it is but neither of us knew much about boats.

Gary woke up in the early afternoon and wanted to know why his boat's stern was nearly level with the waves. We didn't know, nor had we noticed that it was low, so he opened the hatch cover and looked down inside the boat finding it nearly full of water. Coming in to the dock on a wing and a prayer, we made it back to the Coast Guard Station. The bilge pump had failed so the guys spent about half the night installing a new one after the Coast Guard pumped the water from our boat.

Then a storm hit the third day so we came back home. After that first time, every time the three of us went north together, we would nearly get wiped out by storms. The guys tried to say that was why the old time mariners would not sail if a woman was on board ship. I have seen a very tame Lake Michigan turn up with twelve foot waves by the time we got back to shore. It can be really scary.

Gary Huffman (l) and Judy Huffman (r) flank Mickey and me on one of our salmon fishing expeditions on Lake Michigan in the Holly Lynn.

The last time I went with these jokers we were about 17 miles from shore. In the far distance, if we looked really closely, we could see the gray outline of the Sears Tower in Chicago sticking up above the horizon looking to be about an inch tall. It was really faint on the horizon

Suddenly, with absolutely no warning at all, we were hit by a storm that was astonishing in its ferocity. Gary let down the plastic covers behind the captain's chair and told Mickey to steer. Gary started pulling his fishing equipment from the water and handing it inside to me to stow. Mickey was at the wheel steering us back towards Michigan City, full speed ahead. The wind was knocking Gary's expensive fishing poles off the boat like they were toothpicks.

He would get one pole reeled in and hand it to me to place down in the cabin. As I would stick my hand out toward him behind the plastic cover to take hold of another pole, the hail hitting my hand and arm was making blisters form it was hitting me so hard. The screaming of the wind is totally indescribable. I have never heard any noise quite like it in my life.

During all this melee one pole bent down and Gary caught the biggest fish of the day and actually got it on the boat before we started our return trip. When the storm ended 26 minutes later, even though Mickey had been going full speed ahead, we could now see the traffic signals plainly in downtown Chicago. It had blown us backwards several miles.

Gary took back the controls and put Mickey in the bow of the cabin to hold the front end of the boat in the water. He looked over at me and asked me to go below also. My head was down on the

Gary Huffman displays a large salmon he caught
on one of our trips to Lake Michigan.

platform over the cabin steps. He asked me what I was doing. "Go below," he yelled. I told him no, my job was to pray and I was doing a good job of that I can tell you. I just knew if I went below I would drown because that dratted boat would capsize or something and there I would be stuck inside the cabin and the fishes would eat me when we went down. I stayed above board.

We had used a half tank of gas in those 26 minutes the storm lasted and we were the last boat out on the water. When we got within three miles of Michigan City Gary suddenly heard other captains asking about us and got on the radio to tell them we were about out of gas and were having some engine problems. I didn't even know we were having problems with the engines. That would have been the last straw. Two of those captains braved the winds and waves and came out and got one on each side of us and brought us home. I was never so glad to see other people in my life.

I could have kissed the planks in the deck when we landed. I never wanted to see a boat again and to this day have not been on one.

That week I wrote about our adventures and the story ran in the newspaper. I was standing out on the porch of the Democrat building when Dan Marshall, an auctioneer friend of mine, drove up the street. He had read my story and swerved his car toward where I was standing. Dan leaned his head out the open car window and yelled, "Hey, Helen, let's go fishing."

Laughing wildly, Dan drove away. I was the butt of many jokes for my fishing experiences with Mickey and Gary.

Others I Have Known

There have been many others I have known in Van Buren Township over the years. Those people who made such a great impression on me or helped me in many ways over the years have been written about in preceding chapters. However, the ones who came into my life and, like a candle flame burned brightly for awhile, mean a lot to me also. I am including brief notes about some of those people in this chapter.

In this group of residents I include Mary Harris. Mary is a tiny senior citizen who lives not far behind our Beck's Grove property. She has been a loyal friend ever since we moved to this area. Mary will do just about anything for anyone needing help. She spends considerable time assisting the Van Buren Volunteer Fire Department in its fund raising activities. She once rode to Madison with me just for a day out and enthralled me with stories of her childhood growing up in that town.

Mary's husband, Ben, was afflicted with Alzheimer's disease as he aged. Mary took care of Ben for as long as she was physically able to lift and care for him, but during the last year or so of his life he lived at the nursing facility in Nashville. Mary visited with Ben every single day he was in there, assisting him in eating properly, dressing him and assisting the nurses with other patients in any way she could while she was in the facility. This was a remarkable expression of devotion on Mary's part and a good lesson for each of us.

Mary Harris is an energetic, active 86 year old woman who
spends hours in service to others. The woman is never still.

These days she keeps busy in her garden and making doll clothing
for rag dolls the senior citizen club in Bartholomew County make to
give to children who are hospitalized. She also sews pouches that will
eventually contain medical supplies for the Asbury United Methodist
Church of Bartholomew County's overseas mission projects. She has
volunteered at the nursing home in Nashville for the past 15 years and
at the Sycamore Valley Senior Center in Nashville for 25 years.

Then there was Eleanor Clark. She owned a grocery store in
Pike's Peak. I spoke briefly of Eleanor in another chapter.

Eleanor was a kind woman and she knew the financial straits my family was in for a while due to Mickey's heart surgery and us having no health insurance. She had heard me talking about how good my spaghetti and meatballs usually turned out. I explained that my Italian sister-in-law, Bridget, had taught all the women in my family to make it the way the Italians themselves made it.

Pike's Peak Grocery Store which was run by Eleanor Clark. It is now the home of her daughter, Wanda Gordon who operates a beauty shop here.

Eleanor hired me to come to her house, which was attached to her store, and make her a spaghetti and meatball dinner with all the trimmings. While she tended my boys I made her the best batch I possibly could make and it turned out beautifully. I also included a nice salad with three kinds of lettuce, tomatoes, red onion rings and an oil and vinegar dressing that I could make fairly well. To round out the meal I baked her some fresh yeast bread and spread it with garlic butter and toasted it in the oven. I made plenty so she could share it with family or friends or she could store some of it and have it for later meals.

Eleanor paid me $25 to cook that meal for her. In the 1960's this was a lot of money and went far in buying our groceries for a couple of weeks.

Eleanor's daughter Wanda Gordon lives now in the remodeled store building and still maintains a beauty shop in a lower level. Wanda is the sole surviving member of Eleanor's family.

I will never forget Alvin and Ethel McQueary who operated the Jot-Em-Down store at Spurgeon's Corner. Ethel was one of the friendliest women I ever met. No matter how badly she might have been feeling, she always had a smile on her face or would tell me something funny so we could laugh together.

Alvin and Ethel McQueary's family, from left: Alvin, Linda,
Bob, Marge Hovey, Leon and Ethel McQueary.

She was a fellow Kentuckian so maybe this is why I could appreciate her so much. The family moved to Brown County in 1950 from Columbia, Kentucky and took over the operation of the corner grocery. They retired from the grocery business in 1980.

Alvin and Ethel McQueary at home.

Like so many couples in this neighborhood, the McQueary's were married for 68 years. Sadly both are now dead. Ethel died June 4, 1998 and Alvin died September 21, 2000. They are buried in the Rest Haven Cemetery in Edinburgh, Indiana. Many of their descendants still remain in the area.

There was Albert (Pink) Ayers who lived over on Gravel Creek in the next house north of Bud Fleetwood's place. We stopped by his house one chilly fall day for a brief visit and he asked me if I had ever seen a person who had been bitten by a snake and I had to say, that no, I had not.

I had noticed that his pant leg was split to the hip line on his right leg. He pulled the britches leg back and showed me the ugliest leg I had ever seen in my life. It was every color of the rainbow and was swollen enormously, that was why the pant leg had had to be split.

Eleanor and Albert (Pink) Ayers, were former
Gravel Creek Road residents.

Pink had dug his potatoes and placed them in gunny sacks, tied them with a wire and set the sacks in his garage to dry before placing them in his cellar for the winter. When it got to be nearly cold weather he had been moving them into the cellar and thought one of the wires was sticking him on his right thigh. When he looked down he saw seven baby copperhead snakes hanging onto his leg. He drove himself to the hospital for treatment and survived. This was an amazing accomplishment and a wonderful story of fortitude.

On that same road lived Richard and Mary Aspenson. They lived clear to the head of the holler next to the Brown County State Park. Mary worked at various jobs. For awhile she was a gatekeeper at the state park and served as an emergency medical technician for many years. Richard was a truck driver. They had two sons just slightly older than ours named Rick and Randy.

Richard had read about hydroponic gardening and decided to try it. He built two huge greenhouses which were covered with two layers of plastic. Between these layers air was blown for insulation and sturdiness. He grew some of the best lettuce and tomatoes I ever tasted and he had continuous year 'round crops.

He maintained the greenhouses and for five or six years employed several people to help him, one being my friend Mary Harris. An insufficient source of water, difficulty in finding employees and the fact Richard started his own trucking company caused the failure of this experiment, but it was a doozer while it lasted and it was fascinating to observe the process.

Hydroponic gardening is one of several non-polluting businesses that could easily be incorporated into today's economic development plans for this county.

Another good idea is the rearing of buffaloes for table meat. There is one such farm located just east of Bellsville and a second one is just over the line on the same road, but in Bartholomew County.

Not to be omitted are Harry and Norma Crouch. They set up shop as grocery store proprietors in Pike's Peak about the time Eleanor Clark went out of the business. Their store is located about a quarter mile east of where Eleanor's was located.

Originally started as a roadside stand selling hay and dog food, the Crouches listened to their customers and their business grew by leaps and bounds. The roadside stand turned into a permanent building that has been added onto several times as their business continued to grow.

Crouch's Market in Pike's Peak.

One room's walls on the north side of the building are covered with literally hundreds of pictures of people who have frequented the store. Many of them are school pictures of children who liked to come there and shoot pool or play other games with their friends.

Noticing that people liked to snack while they visited the store, the Crouches added hot lunches and bought an ice cream machine for summer time treats. If you asked for an item or could not find it when you came to the store, you can bet the next time you came it would be on the shelf ready for you.

Then they added plumbing supplies for those minor or major household chores and other hardware and in the springtime they sell bulbs and plants for the garden and fertilizer and such.

Norma Crouch today.

Crouch's Market for years has been an official deer and turkey check station. Hunters may bag their deer in Jackson County or even farther away than that but they will bring their kills to Crouch's to be checked in. They love the way Norma takes their bragging pictures and sticks them on her walls to document their prowess in the woods. She will often supply the hunter a copy of the picture and many times will send copies to the newspaper. It has to be one of the busiest check stations in Indiana. For the first time ever, she checked in 110 turkeys this year. Much like the white-tail deer, turkeys have been very successfully seeded back into the county by the conservation officers. The re-seeded bald eagles are also sometimes seen in this area now when they leave their nests along the Monroe Reservoir. What an exhilarating sight that is to see one of these great birds.

The Crouch's success is directly related to their ability to listen to what their customers want. The same can be said for the McQueary's. Once Ethel McQueary left the Jot-Em-Down store it was never as successful as when she operated it. That is until the Crouch's daughter Caroline Knoy operated it. Caroline used the same success formula her parents had used and was very successful. She has since gone out of the grocery business herself and moved to Jackson County but she still assists her parents in the Crouch's Market store on occasion.

When I published my first book, "Appalachian Daughter," Norma stepped right in and threw me a party and sold copies of the books which I autographed for the buyers.

It seems like everything that happens or is reported about Van Buren or its residents finds a place on her walls or in Norma's many albums of Van Buren folklore, history and events.

Here I am at Crouch's Market, signing autographs in my book
Appalachian Daughter. Norma threw me a book launch party.

Harry Crouch is the son of Alfred Ralphy Crouch and Nellie
Crouch. Alfred was named after old Dr. Ralphy at Bellsville and
was nicknamed "Doc".

Harry Crouch as he appears today.

Doc and Nellie raised all kinds of vegetables in what was known as "truck patches" and canned those vegetables under their own label. The vegetables were later trucked and sold to stores in Bloomington. This trip sometimes took two or three days because of the distance and the condition of the roads. Harry continues with the gardening habit and grows many fresh vegetables which are sold directly from the store his wife and daughter operate. He has a strain of potato onions that has been in his family for generations that he continues to propagate.

When Harry was a child he relates how when making kraut, his mother would carve her children's initials on the cabbage stalks and place this marker in the kraut before it was canned. When the can was opened, whichever child's marker was found was given a small special treat. It didn't take much to make a child feel good in those days.

It is rare to find him inside the store as he appears to like working in his huge garden enjoying the outdoors.

Another woman I have known for many years is Joan Birdsong. She is an amazingly talented woman who will be 84 years old on August 4 of this year.

I visited her to take her picture for this book. Without a sign of age she was able to sit on a hard back kitchen chair, draw both legs up onto the chair seat and cross her ankles, perfectly at ease. Most likely if you visit her she will be barefooted since she doesn't like to wear shoes. She looks to be twenty years younger than her actual age.

Joan Birdsong, just a few weeks prior to her 84ᵗʰ birthday.

She began painting at a young age. One of the watercolors she did when she was only 15 years old is now on sale as a print and it is beautiful. She also crochets rag rugs and assembles wild flowers into large bouquets and fashions baskets from various materials, all of which are sold at the Farmer's Market in Bloomington by her son Bob and his wife, Robin.

To keep her mind active and alert she completes crossword puzzles and cryptograms on a daily basis, saying many of them are "too easy."

Joan is the daughter of the late Carl and Marjorie Wilson from Moore's Hill. The Wilsons at one time owned the Old Hickory Tavern in Nashville and lived on Jackson Branch. Nashville businessman Andy Rogers bought the building after Marjorie died and renamed it The Ordinary.

Joan's father wrote the most wonderful poetry I ever read under the pen name of Tramp Starr. His books were called Jokes and Jingles from Curley Shingles and depicted the daily life of country people.

His poetry was run in the Indianapolis Star alongside the photographs taken by Frank Hohenberger, a noted photographer of Brown County and its people. I will include one of his poems titled "Hill Man" at the end of this book. We also featured reprinted poetry in the Brown County Democrat for many years and they were a treat for the readers.

I have saved the best one for last. That man is Michael O'Hara of Bellsville. Michael is a Viet Nam Marine Corps veteran who, during the Tet offensive of 1968, had to wear his clothing so long that when he later removed his field jacket at a rest and recreational center after the offensive ended, he discovered that his clothing beneath the jacket had rotted off his body.

When we were working on erecting the monument in Nashville to the area's veterans, Michael is one of the veterans who assisted me in its construction. He offered so much assistance that I'm not sure we could have succeeded without him.

As a hobby I had for many months been collecting the names of every veteran I could discover from the earliest days of Brown County's history and I wanted to erect a monument for them. It was completed and dedicated in 1992 and did not cost a cent in taxpayer money. Everything that had to do with the monument was donated by the residents of Brown County. Today it is the centerpiece on the courthouse lawn.

In December 1993 I was diagnosed with sepsis (blood poisoning) as a result of having two back surgeries. I had lain in that hospital bed so long that I did not think I would live and it was coming up on Christmas. One of my nurses had slipped up and told me I was in their terminal ward. My fever was raging just below 106 degrees and there was a phone number rattling around in my head. I knew there was something I still needed to do before I died.

I finally gave in and dialed the number. Neither Michael nor anyone outside the family knew how sick I was or that I was near death. He answered the phone and I had to ask him who he was. He told me his name and then it came to me what I needed to talk to him about before I died.

Before I had been admitted to the hospital in early December of that year, I had written a letter to the editor asking for any names that might have been overlooked from that monument and the letters had started coming in while I lay there. The letter I had written had appeared in the newspaper the day I was admitted. Afraid that I would die and this chore would not get accomplished was bearing on my mind I suppose.

Michael said I had called at a good time. "I was just headed out the door for Christmas Eve church services," he told me. "I will turn this over to a higher power."

He must have done so because the next morning, Christmas Day 1993, my fever started its downward spiral for the first time in almost three weeks. The doctor promised me if I could get it down to below 100 degrees for two days I could go home. It continued to go down and I returned to my home just before New Year's Eve.

Michael O'Hara was instrumental in helping me and others in erecting the monument to the veterans on the courthouse lawn in Nashville. He got the high school gymnasium named in honor of Larry Banks and started a local chapter of the Viet Nam Veterans.

The erection of the monument was a success and it was the first of its sort in Brown County. It gave thanks to our county's veterans of all wars and made them proud of their service, even prodding Michael to start a Viet Nam Vet's Organization.

The once almost defunct American Legion and Veterans of Foreign War's groups reorganized and are very active once again. For the first time in its history, Brown County has a full time Veterans Service Officer. It was next to the last county in Indiana to obtain this position.

A new building to house veteran's affairs is being planned for Deer Run Park in Nashville. The new gymnasium at Brown County High School was dedicated as the "Larry Banks Memorial Gymnasium," for Michael's efforts on behalf of his late friend. Larry Banks was the only Brown County man to die in Viet Nam. Larry was the brother-in-law of our own Uncle Oscar Ayers.

When we were preparing for the dedication ceremony of the monument, we learned that there was no trained honor guard unit in the county. I approached the Brown County Sheriff's Department and they got one together for the ceremony. They did a fantastic job and would find they needed the guard when their own members started dying. The veterans followed suit. Now we have trained honor guards from these two sources.

I said this was the first veteran's memorial in Brown County. I erred slightly when I said this. There is a small monument in Pike's Peak in front of the Vivian Lutes home which was erected to honor those who served in the Civil War.

The Civil War Monument has stood sentinel since 1925 in Pike's Peak.

This just goes to show how little acts can have huge successes. All these good things happened for our veterans after we thanked them for their service to their country.

Thanks, guys.

*This is a shot of the old Pike's Peak Post Office and Hendrick's store
which Norma Crouch has kept in her albums of local history.*

*George Bredewater took this aerial view of Pike's
Peak while a friend flew him around.*

George Bredewater captured five of the regulars at the Crouch's Market shooting the breeze one day. He dubbed them the "Pike's Peak Think Tank." It consists of members, from left: Norma Crouch, Doc Beauchamp, Quiller Moore, Jim Wilkerson, and Bob McQueary. Norma is the lone survivor of this group of friends.

Other Little Tidbits

A couple of little notes that I have learned while writing this book included finding a picture of Clarence Blaney and his beautiful milk cow, Aster. Clarence lived up a little holler that runs east off of State Road 135 just north of the Van Buren School. The state would later name this little hamlet Blaneyville to honor this family.

Clarence Blaney stands with his beautiful milk cow,
Aster. Blaneyville was named for this man.

Two Blaney men, Guy and Carl still live today.

At one time there was an official road sign on State Road 135 at each end of the little holler. One sign said, "Blaneyville, Population 7". A couple hundred feet away the sign read, "Blaneyville, Population 11." No one ever tried to explain that little detail to me.

Blaneyville was the first true settlement south of Seelmaer Hill, but there were a few houses before you got that far down the road. The first house south of the big hill was the home of Harry and Wilma Spiker and the next one belonged to the Thomas Shepherd family. Both of these families were related to my husband.

Wilma was a guitar player and singer along with her sister, Hep Beauchamp, Doc Beauchamp, and Louis Henderson. This group started what today is known as the Bean Blossom Bluegrass show which is operated now by the descendants of Bluegrass giant, Bill Monroe.

The Shepherds were our cousins and there were several children in this family. I remember Earl (Red) and his sister, Amaryllis, the best of all I guess. Red used to ride his bicycle everywhere and always pedaled along with one britches leg rolled way up his leg.

*The old Shepherd family home is now vacant after the deaths of
Red and Amaryllis and is in a falling down condition. The old
log structure was typical of the buildings in days gone by.*

The other family who lived near Blaneyville for which I know a
funny story was the Matlock family. Somehow or another we were
related to the Matlocks. If I tried to tell all the genealogies of the
Van Buren residents, it would make each of us our own grandpa's as
the old song goes. They lived on the right just south of Blaneyville
alongside State Road 135 before you came to the "new" Van Buren
School.

When I was a young expectant mother I had a flat tire as I was
on my way up Bellsville Road going for a doctor's examination to
make sure everything was okay. I worked and worked at replacing the
spare, but every time a little pressure was put on the jack, it would fall
down and I had to start all over again. This happened several times

before Noble Matlock, the father of the current older generation of Matlock men and women came along.

Noble Matlock as a young servicemember.

Noble knew who I was, seems like everyone did, but I didn't know all of them. They only had to learn one name (mine) and I had to learn dozens of their names. He took one look at my jack and started laughing. That really didn't help matters. I was running late for the appointment and the steamy summer sun was bearing down. Having someone laugh at me was almost the final straw.

Noble told me he would fix my flat and said that I should go home and have Mickey teach me how to change a tire. "You have the jack upside down," he advised me. The part that was upside down was the post you cranked up by notches but I have no idea to this day what it is called.

Noble and his wife Florence are flanked by their twin daughters, Wanda (l) and Donna (r). Standing behind are their sons, Ray, Teddy, Keith, Rex and Richard (dec. 2006). Ray is the son of Noble and his first wife who died.

The following picture is of the father and mother of Noble Matlock, Sandy and Harriett Matlock.

Sandy and Harriett Matlock were the parents
of Noble Matlock of Blaneyville.

A young Noble Matlock is flanked by his sisters, Vera Hatchet, Mabel Blaney and Hazel Seitz.

When you got to the crossroads at Stone Head you arrived at the grocery store and home of Laurent and Grace Gredy. For many years the Gredy family operated a successful grocery in this location. It was one of the first in the area in the mid 1950s to have a television. When the Indianapolis 500 mile race came on, the store would be filled with the local residents crowding in to watch the race.

*This is a picture of Laurent and Grace Gredy with their two sons,
Lorenzo (L) and John at the elder Gredy's 50ᵗʰ wedding celebration.*

Laurent was from Davos, Switzerland and spoke four languages, German, French, Italian and English. He had a job as a sales representative for a ski manufacturer and traveled extensively, his grandson, Jim Gredy recently told me.

It was while he was on a visit to Indianapolis concerning his company's products that he met the lovely Grace Seelmaer, (who was the aunt of Velma Seelmaer Seitz). Laurent and Grace traveled to New York where she was attending secretarial school and were married there.

The couple returned to Brown County, bought the little store already located at Stone Head, added on to that and operated their grocery until retiring in 1961.

*Photographer George Bredewater captured this
moody shot of Jim Gredy. Jim is a retired teacher
and former Brown County Commissioner.*

Jim Gredy was a county commissioner for several years after he
retired from his teaching job at the Brown County High School in
Nashville. He said he can remember when the only paved road around
was State Road 135. All the others in that area were dusty, rutted gravel
roads. For many years there was no bridge at Stone Head, instead those
traveling along that road had to ford the creek at that location.

Another grandson, Bob Gredy, is an insurance agent in Nashville. Jim and Bob were the sons of Laurent's son Lorenzo Gredy. These two men, whose mother was Geraldine Wilkerson Gredy, are also the grandsons of Jim and Radia Ogle Wilkerson who lived at Pike's Peak.

When our first child Lonnie was born and I showed him to Lonzie, as everyone called Laurent, he said, "Oh, you named him after me. How nice." I never told him any differently because he considered it such an honor to have someone named after him. We had just named him that because it was different and we knew no other Lonnies.

It was in front of this store that my husband lost our shiny red convertible in a flood in 1960. Both the store and home are now gone, but I have seen the flood waters pouring through the windows of the Gredy home at times.

The Stone Head store as it looked long ago. It was torn down by later owners. The home of Laurent and Grace Gredy which stood next door is also gone, destroyed by a tornado in the late 1980s. New structures have now replaced the old.

The Ayers Family

When I started this book I did not mean for it to become just another book about my family or a memoir. I wanted to highlight the lives of the truly wonderful people I had come to know and love in Van Buren Township, but with this style of writing it becomes very difficult not to insert information about your own family since each one is so intertwined with all the others.

I have already written a separate story about the Scott Ayers family. He was Mickey's next younger brother. There was another, much younger brother named Richard (now deceased) and an older sister named Esther Gayle (Pud).

Lenore Ayers with her four children, from left, Scott, Pud and Richard. Mickey is peering over Richard's head.

Richard married Rebecca (Becky) Reed and they had two children, Jimmy and Sandra Dee. I introduced Richard and Becky and they hit it off right away, marrying not many months later. After 30 years of marriage, Richard died while in his early 50s. He had been dead just over a year when I introduced Becky to my brother Jimmy who had just recently lost his wife to cancer, and within five weeks of meeting they married. I laughingly tell Becky I just can't get rid of her. She must have been meant to be my sister-in-law since she has been one twice; first to Mickey's brother, then to mine. She is a fine woman who takes wonderful care of my brother.

Becky was a member of the Herschell and Grace Reed family that moved into the farmhouse we vacated when our new home in Copperhead Hollow was completed. This Reed family had, at one time, 18 children, but by the time we got acquainted with the family it had shrunk to a somewhat more manageable size. Remember how in another chapter I told about children's deaths during epidemics? This family lost four children in seven days just before they moved to our neighborhood. Becky said recently all four children died of Rocky Mountain spotted fever, which I believe is caused from the bite of wood ticks and is very quick acting. The husband of one of my cousins, while performing his job as a conservation officer in another state, was bitten by one of these ticks and died within three days.

Prior to moving near us, the Reed family had lived in a pretty heavily wooded area of Jackson County and that is where the children died. Nowadays the family has become much smaller still as more and more of these children die off, many with some type of lung problem which also afflicts Becky, but she is working hard to overcome the effects of the illness.

Esther Gayle "Pud" was married first to Bill Jackson and they had children, Gary, Dean and Cindy. They divorced and she married Jim McConnell and they adopted a daughter, Jamie. They also divorced and she married Jay Watkins who died several years ago of cancer. Pud has recently had a couple of strokes and is now residing at the nursing home in Nashville.

According to Weston Goodspeed's History of Brown County there was an "Old Man Jackson" who was a water well driller in the very earliest days of Brown County. Our brother-in-law Bill would have been a direct descendant of this man, probably several great grandsons down the line, but still a descendant. Goodspeed did not list the man's first name nor where he came from but I bet he was also from Kurtz (my childhood home) where most of the Jackson's lived for many years, practicing their well drilling craft.

Water well drilling is one of those crafts passed down from father to son to grandson, etc. I never met a Jackson man who could not "witch" or "douse" as some prefer to call it, and who did not drill for water.

Mickey learned the trade while his sister was married to Bill and both our boys and I can witch for water and Mickey was also a well driller for nearly 40 years. Lonnie and Douglas both know the trade but for the present time have decided not to pursue it. They did operate our business one whole summer in 1977 while still students in high school while their dad was a deputy sheriff.

*Mickey Ayers as he appeared as a teenager learning the well
drilling profession from his brother-in-law Bill Jackson.*

Mr. Goodspeed explains that if you wanted a water well drilled
you had to do it while Old Man Jackson was in your neighborhood.
Otherwise, it could be a long time getting him to come back to your
property.

According to Goodspeed, each person wanting a well put down
had to go to wherever Old Man Jackson had lastly been drilling. It
would be up to you to furnish the mule or horsepower to move his

machine, which would have been mounted on sled runners most likely, and drag it to your place. You also had to provide good vittles (food) and give him a place to sleep.

The next person needing his services would then take him off your hands and so it went from house to house in those days.

It was while Pud was married to Bill Jackson that my husband learned to drill water wells and he would follow that profession for about 40 years. During the summer of some of Mickey's high school years he lived with his sister in Greene County and learned the trade while working with Bill. Mickey bought his own rig in 1968 and retired in 2006. We had the two sons, Lonnie and Douglas, both of whom I seem to mention a lot in these little stories. Lonnie lives in Barcelona, Spain and Douglas lives in Tokyo, Japan. We also have a grandson and a granddaughter who are Lonnie's children. Douglas had a son, George, who died when he was 11 on Good Friday, 2004. He had been totally disabled his whole life.

Donald and Lenore Ayers were the parents of these four siblings. As I talked with local residents about this book they wanted to make sure that I included something about the family I married into.

The Ayers family except for Gayle: Mickey, Lenore, Aunt Mary
(Oscar's wife) Scott, and Donald is holding Richard.

Donald was one of three sons of Arnold and Myrtie Ayers. His brothers were Arnold Oscar and Glen Bernell. His sister was Anna (Ann) Elizabeth. Bernell and Ann are mentioned in other chapters. Bernell died in 1956, Ann in 1976 and Donald in 1977. Oscar, or OJ as we call him, survives

Oscar Ayers today.

Oscar Ayers while serving in the U.S. Army
in Korea during the early 1950's.

Granddad Arnold, died in 1961, and Granny (Myrtie) died in 1979. Both are buried at Mt. Zion Cemetery.

The Arnold Ayers family in days gone by. Included are from
left: Myrtie, Arnold, Bernell, Don, Ann and Oscar.

My mother taught me that if I didn't have anything good to say about somebody, don't open my mouth. So that is about all the background I can give you on the Ayers family because I feuded with one of them over the years. So rather than say anything bad, I will give two instances of my admiration for Donald. He served his time on Okinawa when he was already the father of four children and was nearly 40 years old. Also, he was the father of my husband and for that gift alone I will always be grateful.

Lenore was an easier woman for me to get to know. She was a very smart woman and went back to high school, earned her GED and then went into college when she was in her 50s to earn her Associate's degree. After that she became a Head Start school teacher and loved every minute she spent working with these young children helping to develop their minds.

She was also a gifted sculptor and artist, producing many yard ornaments from the blue clay that Donald brought up from far underground when he was drilling water wells. She would sit with him some days while he was working and grab up a handful of this gooey clay (we called it blue soapstone) and start shaping it into animal figurines. That evening she would take it home and place it inside her oven on a pan and harden it. Once it was completely dried she would then paint the figures with waterproof paint and give them to her children and grandchildren to enjoy. They could be placed outdoors and would last several months. Had she fired them in a kiln they probably would have lasted much longer, but she did not own a kiln so she made do. She sculpted deer, rabbits, squirrels, ducks and geese.

Lenore loved to work in oil paints and her art was much like that of Grandma Moses' primitive style and included lots of little details that were not always obvious at first glance. I have one painting of hers hanging in my living room and I swear every time I glance at it I see another detail I had overlooked. She never entered any of her artworks into competition, painting only for her own enjoyment.

While teaching the Head Start kids she made her own version of homemade Play Dough and many other things to supplement her teaching materials. The government grants to teach these young children only stretched so far, thus she went into her kitchen, and produced many teaching tools and toys for her kids at her own expense. She really loved these children.

To make your own play dough combine: 2 cups flour, 2 tablespoons olive oil; 1 teaspoon powdered alum; 1 cup salt; 1 cup water and various food colors.

Dissolve the dry ingredients completely in water and oil, and then knead the ingredients until the colors are uniform. Store the product in a tightly closed plastic bag or sealed jar. By using various shades of food coloring you can let the kids experiment to their heart's content.

Lenore Ayers in her later years.

She taught these young kids many simple little songs and dances and read them dozens of short stories to improve their speech and motor skills and so they could gain an appreciation for the printed word.

Lenore was one of three children of Lizzie and Grover Wilkerson and she attended the Story school. She had two brothers Clifford, deceased, and Amos, now 83. It was during her seventh grade year that she won the school's spelling bee and received a commendation from the Louisville Times newspaper. She graduated the eighth grade of Story school in 1932.

Lenore's certificate for winning the Story School spelling bee in 1931.

*Lenore's diploma for graduating from the
eighth grade of Story School in 1932.*

Lenore became very vexed with me while I worked at the Brown County Democrat for writing a story about the high incidence of cancer around the Story area. I had suddenly sat back one day after burying another friend (Bud Fleetwood), and realized that more than half the people I knew in Van Buren Township had died of one form of cancer or another.

Dr. Robert Seibel was the county health doctor at the time, and he and the Indiana Chapter of the American Cancer Society agreed with me but when we met to discuss the issue they wanted me to do the research to prove it. Since I was working five days a week at a very demanding job, I just could not see my way clear to doing this much research so it never got done. It was sad irony when Lenore died of lung cancer and her son Richard died in his early 50s from multiple forms of cancer.

If the residents of this area did not die from cancer, a huge number of them lived to be well into their nineties or even more than 100 years old.

The oldest former residents were George Anthony, 109, and his son, Cloyd Anthony, who lived to be 103. They came from the area at the junction of Gravel Creek and Elkinsville Road and both were school teachers. Today there are several members of this community who are in the mid to late 90s.

Mickey's "grandmother" was Pauline Anthony who was married to Bert Anthony, another of George's sons.

While I worked at the newspaper we had a woman working there who went to the counter one day when a very elderly gentleman came in to renew the subscription for his father. Lynn looked Cloyd Anthony right in the eye and said, 'You have to be (expletive) me. How old is your father?" Cloyd explained to her that he himself was only 86 and his father was 104 at that time I believe. Cloyd would live many years after that visit to our office.

Both George and Cloyd (as did several others including Odon Carmichael) used to write me little notes on their renewal notice cards asking how everyone was doing. Each time George was in town he would stop by the newspaper and tell me hello. I wish I had kept their notes, but alas, I am a tosser.

The Ayers Family Photo Album

Ann Elizabeth Ayers
stands before an old barn.
She was the daughter of
Arnold and Myrtie Ayers.

Donald Ayers is shown
in a yellowed newspaper
photograph demonstrating
the old-time art of witching
for water. He used bent
wires in a pop bottle
for handles; I used a
forked dogwood stick

Myrtie and her daughter
Ann Ayers are shown
with a touching
demonstration of love

Myrtie Ayers

A second picture of
Myrtie Ayers.

This is our sons
Lonnie (seated) and
Douglas in 1978.

The Schools and Churches

At one time there was a school located every couple of miles in the more populous places around Van Buren but after the purchase of the land for the Brown County State Park, Yellowwood Forest; Monroe Reservoir and the Hoosier National Forest most of the schools and churches disappeared along with most of the residents of this area.

The old Mt. Zion Church. It has long been gone from the local landscape. A shelterhouse now stands where the church once stood.

From an original once upon a time count of 23 schools and numerous churches, only one school and a handful of churches survive in Van Buren Township today. There is only one school (Van Buren, grades K-6) and the following six churches still standing and being used today. The list of churches includes: Mt. Nebo, Christiansburg, Beck's Grove, Grandview, Pikes Peak and Bellsville.

I have tried to make a list of the schools that at one time served as the educational foundation for the children of Van Buren Township. With the assistance of retired educator Bud Brand who had a copy of former superintendent of schools Warren Ogle's book, *Brown County Indiana Schools*, we were able to arrive at the following names of the Van Buren Township schools: Gravel Creek; Story; Van Buren; Beck's Grove; Pikes Peak and Bellsville. Mr. Ogle (Louise Fleetwood's dad) is long deceased but many of his family still remain in Brown County.

Also making the list was: No. One School; Kelp; Valley Branch; Christiansburg; Mt. Nebo; Grandview; Spurgeon's and Mt. Zion schools. Only one school remains today and that is the Van Buren Elementary School now located just north of Stone Head on State Road 135. This is not the same Van Buren School originally noted by Mr. Ogle. The old one contained grades one through 12 and could be better described as Christiansburg and was demolished.

Other schools in the same general area, but located in then Johnson Township, are included here because those areas later became a part of either Van Buren or Washington Township depending upon their location. After the reservoir filled with water Johnson Township no longer existed. The properties lying east of the reservoir now belonged in Van Buren Township; the ones on the west side of the lake became Washington Township properties. Schools included were: Deckard; Crooked Creek; Axsom Branch; and Dewar Ridge on the Washington Township side and Elkinsville, Blue Creek and Browning schools on the Van Buren side.

The new Van Buren Elementary School at Stone Head was completed and bus routes assigned to bring the children to one location just before 1960. My husband graduated from Van Buren High School at Christiansburg in 1956 and it closed after the 1958 school year, and I moved here in 1960. It was during those two intervening years that the new elementary school was completed at Stone Head.

Once the Monroe Reservoir was built and had filled with water there was a silence from many of the school play yards.

No bells rang to call the students to classes; no shrill children's voices could be heard in the classrooms or on the play yards; no slap...slap...slap of a jump rope could be heard beating the ground outside the building. The swings in the play yard now swayed gently in a passing breeze, turning upon themselves, tangling their chains, if, that is, someone had not already taken them away also.

The teachers, even knowing the classrooms that held so many memories of so many students and their activities were doomed for destruction, erased the blackboards carefully for the last time and carefully placed the eraser and chalk in the apron of the blackboard. They packed up their teaching materials, turned to take one last look around with teary eyes and locked the front door as they left their buildings. In the eerie silence remaining after they left one could hear the steady clank and screech of the iron bulldozer's cleated tracks as it prepared to destroy this part of Van Buren's children's lives.

Mr. Brand did not know where two of the schools Mr. Ogle listed in his book were actually located. Those two were the Salem and Oak Ridge Schools. But according to the map Mr. Ogle provided, it appears that the Oak Ridge School was somewhere along Berry

Ridge in the extreme southern reaches of the township, although Mr. Brand does not recall it.

*The old Bellsville School still stands today and
is part of the Ron Schuster Art Studio.*

Some of these schools served only a handful of children. In the Elkinsville book, *"The Town That Was"* some of these little schools showed only a dozen or so students enrolled in some years and they appeared to be from only two or three families. The enrollment at the larger schools like the Elkinsville School was much higher.

If these little country schools had a good teacher, and many of them did, the quality of the education gained by the pupils was excellent. In reading the book about Elkinsville I saw the names of many teachers who bore the Deckard family name. Many of these siblings became excellent teachers. I had one of them, Cora, as my sixth grade teacher at the Clearspring School in Jackson County and he was a terrific and capable teacher. Now far advanced in years, Mr. Deckard lives in the nearby Jackson County community of Houston.

My sixth grade teacher was Cora Deckard. Here he is still fairly active on his farm in Houston at the age of 91.

The schools in this area sent citizens out into the world to become doctors and nurses, lawyers, judges, teachers, artisans, writers and into many other professional areas. They also produced a large number of perfectly ordinary citizens like most of us who went on to become solid contributors to society and raised their families in the manner in which they had been taught. These men and women worked hard, showed strong work ethics and prospered. Nearly all would look back on their educational beginnings with fond memories.

The small township schools, long gone today, served a huge population of young people over the decades in which they existed.

Nearly all were built of a simple white clapboard construction with a belfry for the school bell. Some, however, were built without the belfry and served a much smaller group of children.

Two of these schools are still in use today. This list includes the Story and Bellsville.

The Story School building was moved to Spurgeon's Corner on down State Road 135 from Story about five miles. This school house stood just about across the road from where Penny Tolle's house stands today. It has been used as a grocery store at Spurgeon's Corner by various families over the years. Originally it was called the Jot-Em-Down Store and the original proprietors were Alvin and Ethel McQueary. Upon the retirement from the grocery business of these two truly remarkable individuals it was operated by a half dozen or so other families and has had several names. Most of the old-timers still refer to the store as the Jot-Em-Down store. And, it is only the old timers who remember it was once the Story school house.

The second school, Bellsville, is now the shop for a glass artisan.

For an excellent documentation of these township schools please refer to the very entertaining and enlightening book, *"Brown County*

Indiana Schools—A Half Century," produced by the late teacher and school superintendent Warren Ogle, published in 1993. The book lists the schools, gives a map for locating the schools and lists many of the pupils and other demographic data of this area.

Mr. Ogle speaks of the county school superintendent Grover G. Brown. To graduate from school every child was required to write a perfectly composed letter to Grover Brown. He would respond to each one with corrections and they would resubmit their letters until they got it just right. Mr. Brown also talked to each of the classes and told them the tale of the "Taleypo," which meaning seems to now be lost, but never forgotten by the former students in these small schools. I was lucky enough to receive a picture from Maxine Hedrick of a very young Mr. Brown and his sister, Eathel Brown Bradley. I believe it was this Mrs. Bradley's chamber pot I confiscated while living in Sheila Lucas' farmhouse.

Mr. Ogle, describes the early log construction, size of the building, how they were lighted and heated, how the blackboards were painted on the walls; the recitation benches, costs of building the schools, the pay rates of the teachers and how they were trained and hired and other delights about these early schools which fed the receptive minds of the earliest settler's children to this area.

As poorly as they were constructed, and some had dirt floors according to Mr. Ogle, these little township schools produced an amazing number of very intelligent professionals who went on out into the world and became teachers, principals and superintendents of other much larger school systems, not only in Indiana, but across the world.

*A very young Grover G. Brown and his sister, Eathel Brown
(Bradley). They lived on Gravel Creek, Maxine Hedrick told me.
In his later years he was the county school superintendent.*

The Pike's Peak School, circa 1930. Hiram Brand was the teacher.

Christiansburg School, 1943-44. Hiram Brand was the teacher.

Pike's Peak School, 1939-40. Hiram Brand was the teacher.

Van Buren High School, Class of 1943. Paul Roush was their teacher.

These little churches and schools fed the souls and the minds of the residents. They were the official meeting places for many events such as pie suppers, spelling bees, dinners on the ground, church/baptismal services and burials. In the much earlier years of this township, many of these schools served as meeting places for churches also.

Some of the churches were served by circuit riding preachers and only a few had a minister dedicated just to that one church. A minister might ride his horse or drive his horse and buggy, later perhaps a car, to various churches at two different hours on Sunday, or staggering the visits to every other Sunday, thus earning the name circuit rider.

The old Harmony Baptist Church has now been
replaced with a very modern version.

Attending church services was the highlight of the week for many of the country residents. Despite the hardships they endured every day of the week, sitting in church on Sundays lifted their spirits above their deprivations. Here, in these tiny country churches, they could lift their eyes to the Lord and their voices in song.

The burdens of deprivation, poverty and want could be laid down outside by the church door before they entered the Lord's house. If they still felt like carrying those burdens after the sermon, they could pick them up as they left His house.

It was there in these small churches amidst the glorious sounds of Amazing Grace and other wonderful old-time hymns they learned how to live their lives in the way the Lord wanted them to lead it. As they gave their hearts and lives into the hands of their Lord they learned about salvation of their eternal souls. They ensured that When the Roll was Called up Yonder, they would be there.

This is a recent picture of the Christiansburg United Methodist Church which is an excellent example of country style architecture.

Hill Man

Written by Tramp Starr and published in 1941
(Reprinted by Permission)

I would not give the quiet of these hills,
For all the wonders that the cities hold,
Or trade one peaceful day their presence fills
For all the world's mad scramble after gold—
For green hills, where the leafy forests wave,
And sleepy valleys drowsing in the sun,
Have ever held me bound, a willing slave,
Their need bred in my blood when life begun.

I would not give this small white house of mine,
For any that your towns could offer me,
Or trade one blooming field, at evening time,
For years on end of wealth's security—
For tinkling cow bells, when the sun has set,
The mocking bird's late song, the whippoorwills,
Are things my country heart could not forget,
If I should lose the quiet of the hills.

I would not give the music that I know
For any famous orchestra or band,
Or trade one patting foot and scraping bow,
For all the other music in the land—
For "Turkey in the Straw" and "Money Musk"
Stir memories of half-forgotten thrills—
A dance at Wilson's barn—a starlit dusk,

And music lying soft among the hills.

I would not give one friend I own today,
For dozens I might gain in some far place,
Or have them changed in any single way,
In mode of dress, or speech, or smiling face—
For I have found them staunch when trouble fell,
And kindly as the hills that gave them birth—
Nowhere are men that I could love so well,
In bright and crowded places of the earth.

I would not give these gracious hills I own,
My house, and blooming fields and winding lane,
Or one tried friend, whom I have always known,
For any gift of gold, or worldly gain—
For I have found life's quiet paths are best,
A mocking bird at dawn and whippoorwills—
Calm hours to mark long days, and peaceful rest,
When darkness closes down upon the hills.

The End (Maybe, Maybe Not)

Did you enjoy meeting and visiting with my friends in their homes and learning of their daily lives? I sure hope you enjoyed reading about their exploits and their triumphs. Weren't they wonderful people? Do you need some more coffee, cookies, anything at all? No? Do you really have to go so soon? Well, come on back for another visit next year. This rocking chair and the logs on the grate will be right here waiting for your return. I plan to write about my many artistic friends in the next book. I have tentatively titled the third in this trilogy, The Artisans of Van Buren. See you next year, you hear?

Order Form

If you enjoyed reading this book and would like to order additional copies as gifts, or you would like to receive a copy of my first book in this series, "Appalachian Daughter," please return this form along with a money order to:

Helen Ayers-Books
7256 Keith Donaldson Road
Freetown, IN 47235

_____ **Appalachian Daughter** @ $17.00 ea = _____
Copies

_____ **The Stuff of Legends** @ $25.00 = _____
Copies

SAVE $3. Order both books and pay only one postage. A great gift idea.

A third book in this series, "The Artisans of Van Buren" is planned to be available next year. Please watch for news about its release.

Thank you for buying and reading my books. I hope you have a marvelous time with them. I always thought history could and should be related to students in an amusing fashion. I hope you think that I have accomplished my goal.

A Note to My Readers

I especially enjoy hearing from my readers. E-mail me at helenayers40@hotmail.com. Please send me your comments and include the word **BOOKS** on the subject line or it will be deleted without being read.

About the Author

The author signing books at her first book launch.

Mrs. Ayers is always surprised to realize she is writing historical non-fiction since history was her worst subject while in school. She thought the subject could have been written with a bit of flair, humor and satire as well as just the boring facts, and she's always hoping she has succeeded in presenting her subject matter in a more interesting light. She lives in Southern Brown County Indiana with her husband and three little dogs, Jake, Goldie and Beau.

21213436R00217

Made in the USA
Lexington, KY
08 March 2013